BRAVE NEW CHILD

BRAVE NEW CHILD
Education for the 21st Century

Copyright © 1989
by Terrence Webster-Doyle
(all rights reserved)

(alphabetically)
Production Coordinator:
Kathy Des Prez

Cover Design:
Robert Howard

Editor, Cover Bird, Book Design:
Charlene Koonce

Art Direction:
John Shoolery

Creative Consultant:
Jean Webster-Doyle

Word Processing:
I'm Your Type

Published by:
Atrium Publications
Post Office Box 938
Ojai, California 93023
(805) 646-0488
or (800) 432-5566 for book order information

ISBN 0-942941-06-3

These are the thoughts of all men in all ages
and lands, they are not original with me.
If they are not yours as much as mine, they are
nothing or next to nothing.
If they do not enclose everything, they are
next to nothing.
If they are not the riddle and the untying of
the riddle, they are nothing.
If they are not just as close as they are distant,
they are nothing.

— Walt Whitman
from *Leaves of Grass*

Table of Contents

Brave New Child — *Education for the 21st Century* is the second in a series of books on psychological conditioning entitled ***The Sane and Intelligent Living Series***. The first book of the series, **Growing Up Sane** — *Understanding the Conditioned Mind*, focuses on the destructive nature of psychological conditioning by examining its influence on our social structures and its root within the psyche itself. This second book in the series, **Brave New Child**, examines a solution to the problem of psychological conditioning. The third and fourth books in the series are: **The Religious Impulse** — *A Quest for Innocence*, which contrasts contradictory religious practices with the religious mind, free of conditioning; and **Peace, The Enemy of Freedom** — *The Myth of Nonviolence*, an enquiry into the paradoxical nature of creating peace.

Forthcoming books include: **Atrium** — *The Foundation of Learning*; **Student to Student** — *Conversations on War and Peace*; **Teacher to Teacher** — *Conversations on Education and Freedom*; and **The Child in Changing Times** — *A Curriculum on Psychological Conditioning.*

Each book, although part of a series, is complete in itself. The focus of all the books is to examine the nature and structure of conflict — inwardly and outwardly. Each book offers a different perspective on this theme.

FOREWORD
Education for the 21st Century
A Crisis in Learning

Education in the 20th Century has primarily been concerned with training students to survive in an emerging industrialized world, providing skills which produce goods and ensure economic prosperity — or, in essence, physical survival. Although scientific thinking has given us relative freedom and security, it has also created a life threatening technology of highly sophisticated war machinery. It appears that our highly developed intellectual capacity is out of balance with a mature understanding of how to use that intellect in humane ways.

Technological thinking has freed and enslaved us. We are caught in a seemingly endless, voracious consumption which has divided humans at every level. This divisive, fragmentary, competitive way of life has created and sustained conflict for thousands of years. Before the 20th Century, mankind was able to endure this conflict because it was limited to isolated parts of the world. However, the 20th Century has brought us to the point where conflict is a *global* threat, a real, eminent and urgent matter that concerns every human being.

It is now imperative that we turn our attention to education by helping young people not only to survive technologically and economically, but also to see the origin of conflict within themselves and society. We need to help them understand how technological and economic survival, because it has become divorced from psychological survival, creates and sustains destructive and competitive relationships.

The 21st Century must develop an education for learning about ourselves and our relationships if we are to survive psychologically and, hence, socially. At the core of learning about ourselves in relationship is understanding psychological conditioning — what it is, how it forms our attitudes and behavior, and how it fundamentally creates conflict in living. The issue of psychological conditioning is perhaps the greatest threat to humankind's existence, since it underlies our personal and social disorder. We urgently need to address this crisis in learning, this issue of psychological conditioning, for we now have the technological capability to bring about immense global suffering.

Our schools need to educate young people not only intellectually, but also in understanding the nature and structure of conflict which resides in the process of thinking. We need to examine the limitations of knowledge, and the difference between technological (or scientific) thinking and psychological thinking aimed at bringing about change in behavior. Education for the 21st Century has as its challenge the bringing about of enquiry into the roots of our disorder, understanding the place of the intellectual capacity in creating a world free of conflict.

INTRODUCTION
Freedom from
Psychological Conditioning

Are schools conditioning children through a system of rewards and punishments to compete against each other? Are schools imposing a hierarchical structure, a psychological and social pecking order, that produces leaders and followers? When we compare one child to another, or when we condition a child to emulate heroic images in order to make him conform, to be "good," are we not creating a divided child — one who will be at war with himself (or herself) psychologically? When we condition a child by asking him to indisputably pledge allegiance to a flag, a symbol representing a political fragment, are we not destroying that child's intelligence and adding more conflict in relationship? Could young men, right out of high school, have gone to war and killed men, women and children if they had not been indoctrinated by political conditioning? Is what we call "socialization" in our schools merely a form of propaganda that conditions our children to act individually, nationalistically and aggressively towards the rest of humanity?

The intention of **Brave New Child** is to question the conventional process by which we rear and educate children so that we can begin to understand how education contributes to creating conflict in relationship. This book examines the psychological structure of the conditioned mind, a mind educated to live life according to idealistic patterns of behavior established by society and reinforced through the numerous social and educational situations created out of this conditioning. The intent of this book and the series is to enquire into how and why psychological conditioning comes into being and to explore the destructive nature of its influence — both individually and socially.

As stated earlier, psychological conditioning is the most important challenge to affect mankind. It is the foundation of endless social strife, the primary cause of war, and that which underlies many of humanity's diseases. Psychological conditioning touches our everyday lives; it controls our actions and is the content of our dreams. Affecting how people relate, it forms our attitudes about life and relationship. Generating endless beliefs by which we live, it creates an isolating, fragmentary world.

Understanding psychological conditioning is our greatest challenge in living, yet conditioning is *not* well understood. This is truly frightening since we are involved every day in conditioning our children and each other. The family, school, church, home, business, culture and nation are all agents of conditioning. We want these agencies to serve this purpose; we want to be conditioned and crave the security and comfort it appears to give us.

What is psychological conditioning? How does it come about? Why do we condition ourselves and our children? Is it possible to live a life free of conditioning? Can we see the terrible danger of conditioning, and therefore see the need to understand it? Do we ever seriously think about these questions? My hope is that this and other books that deal straightforwardly with psychological conditioning will awaken us to the influences in society that are conditioning us so that we can begin to address this issue as a part of our daily lives. I would also like to see psychological conditioning become the primary focus in the curriculum of our schools, to help young people understand and be free of its destructive influence.

The first book of this series, **Growing Up Sane**, graphically illustrates the problem of psychological conditioning by exploring the paradoxical nature of traditional education, child rearing, and the structures we have created in society to mold behavior.

Brave New Child, the second book in the series, discusses a solution to the problem of psychological conditioning. Part I examines how we approach solving problems, discusses the nature of enquiry and intelligence, and lays the foundation for the rest of the book.

Part II explores a *new* education, one that fosters a young person's understanding of the personal and social influences of psychological conditioning.

Part III explores the need for self-discovery at a fundamental level, observing the deepest roots of conflict.

A sample curriculum is presented in Part IV for parents and teachers interested in developing activities that demonstrate to young people the nature and structure of conditioning. These specific exercises are a mirror in which a child can see the state of his mind reflected, enhancing observation of his own behavior. (In a forthcoming companion book to **Brave New Child**, a comprehensive curriculum for parents and teachers on the issue of psychological conditioning will be presented.)

Part V discusses the use of Martial Arts training to help children understand the nature and structure of violence. This training provides a unique context for solving conflict nonviolently.

Part VI is a section of commentaries written for parents, teachers and students on a variety of fundamental issues concerning the education of the brave new child, issues generally not talked about yet vital to understanding ourselves. **Brave New Child** concludes with the same question proposed in **Growing Up Sane**: "Where do we go from here?"

Before reading Part I, it is important to be aware of the intention of the particular format used. The presentation is not in the conventional prose style. Most books on the philosophy of education or educational reform are generally written in the conventional way that we have been taught to write in school; this method presents a statement, an hypothesis, and then substantiates the statement by logical reasoning, often referring to other like-minded thinkers. The danger of this approach is that it contributes to the intellectual information or knowledge about an issue but often does not lead to any real insight. Our brains have been conditioned to gather knowledge, to analyze and synthesize that knowledge, and then to create a "solution" to the "problem." In the field of technology or science, this is appropriate. However, in the realm of understanding psychological conditioning or changing human behavior, this analytical, linear, intellectual approach only compounds the problem due to the nature and structure of thinking as a form of measurement. [This condition is explored in **Growing Up Sane** and will be explored further in **Brave New Child**.]

The format of Part I has been carefully chosen so that unnecessary information and analysis about psychological conditioning is not generated. Instead, Part I contains independent observations into the nature and structure of psychological conditioning, one observation per page so one can consider each carefully with leisure. This format allows the presentation of insights in a simple, nonintellectual way. It is so easy to intellectualize what is being said, to absorb information and store it as knowledge for future reference. *However, what is important here is to use these observations as catalysts to create insight so one can observe oneself.*

These observations are often presented as questions to raise doubts about how we conventionally educate children. This format is used to create space to reflect, question, and creatively doubt, to hold the intellectual mind back from reacting too quickly by judging content. This is the nature of observation. It brings our conditioned ways into the light so we can see them exactly as they are, without interpretation. There can be resistance to observing our lives directly. We may want to think about and analyze our actions; observation can seem too simplistic and childish to the overeducated mind. Presenting observations without reference to any academic, political or religious authority is dismissed as uneducated opinion by many people. This view blocks simple observation of our daily lives and direct understanding of ourselves.

Observation is perception, actual perceiving in the moment. It is insight into reality. Observation is not conjecture or opinion, nor is it theory or any form of idealism. It is simply what is. This does not mean that the observations presented here are The Truth. Either they are accurate perceptions of what is actually occurring and therefore true, or they are not accurate and therefore untrue. The point is that they are not meant to be conclusions or assertions to be accepted or rejected.

The nature of these, or any, observations is to stimulate awareness in others. A person sees something of concern and uses words to express the observation; the intent is that another person will also see and understand what is expressed. The word is not the thing; the description is not the actual observation. What is so very important is to see, to be aware, to accurately observe, and to have immediate insight into psychological conditioning. Understanding and, hence, freedom from conditioning cannot come through time. Analysis, intellectualization, thought are in time.

As stated, these observations are presented without reference to like-minded thinkers. The reader's mind may compare what is being said to similar statements written by others in the past, but such comparisons are dangerous for they breed conflict. So, can we reflect on each observation and see the truth or falseness of it, without analyzing or comparing it to what authorities say? Can we simply look for ourselves and, in so doing, awaken our capacity for insight, for real intelligence? The reader may not consider this book with its seemingly oversimplified "observations" to be important or worthy of serious consideration. But is understanding ourselves only the privilege of the academic, psychological, political or religious authority? And even if they understand an issue beyond their own specialized, fixed viewpoint, what good does that do us? In other words, we still have to examine for ourselves. To understand psychological conditioning means to understand who and what we are, in each moment, through direct observation.

If we are truly interested in creating a healthy life for our children and ourselves, we must understand this fundamental issue of psychological conditioning. It seems that no one is completely free from conditioning and, tragically, very few recognize or understand its danger — individually or globally. The intent of this book and this series is to bring about a *new child*, a child capable of living intelligently, of living a wholly different life than children live now. The intent of **Brave New Child** is to share a fundamental insight into the root of psychological conditioning that can radically free humanity from its terrible conflicts in relationship.

[**Please Note:** This book primarily uses "he," "him," or "his" to denote *human being* and is not intended to assert male superiority. Using "he/she," "him/her" or "his/hers" continually is obviously awkward, and there is not yet a satisfactory term in English that encompasses both genders. I apologize to the reader who is offended by this usage and suggest that we look at how conditioning has affected the development of our language — and how language, in turn, affects our attitudes.]

Author's Note

The word *intention* is important to understand in reading this book. Intention, or intent, means "to direct the eyes or mind, to set out on one's course." It is my intention to direct the mind to observe what is occurring in life without the imposition of any psychological authority. Since we *are* conditioned, it seems difficult to keep one's eyes or mind directed in this way, to set out and keep one's course in a straight line, so to speak. There are many forces that pull at us and keep us in our prisons of conditioning. However, as one sees the necessity and seriousness of observing one's conditioning, this activity takes on a life and strength of its own. At first this life is fragile and weak, and conditioning seems to dominate one's actions. However, the more one's "eyes" and mind become directed, the more opportunity there is for freedom.

In this book I intend to demonstrate the force of conditioned thinking and its destructive nature. This doesn't mean that I am completely free of conditioning. In fact, the opposite seems true; as I look and write, my own conditioning is thrown into ever bolder relief. There are times when I feel overwhelmed by its power as I witness myself reacting in a conditioned way. Sometimes these reactions are frightening because of their intensity. But most of the time I feel that something is being deeply affected by my growing awareness — loosened up, so to speak. Something is moving.

Understanding conditioning is not an intellectual "game." It is very real! And dangerous! From an early age I have been struggling with conditioned living. I could not keep up with what was expected of me. In school I "failed" miserably and was always trying to escape. I also tried to avoid church for there too I felt a heavy weight. And in the armed forces I finally fell apart; the questioning of my conventional life created a temporary collapse. It took me years to understand what had happened, what conditioning was, and how it was fundamentally affecting everything I was involved in. I was challenged to find out what caused this destructive state of mind. It became a matter of life and death. The challenge remains; the intention is greater than ever as I see more clearly to the root of conditioning.

I share in this book *original* insights, original meaning "belonging to the origin; new, fresh; coming from the source." These are observations that I have seen for myself. The way I communicate, the style of writing, is not important. Also, I am not interested in comparing what is written herein to any other author for comparison breeds conflict. What I feel *is* important is to see for oneself, for this is the only thing one can *really* do. As long as one's intention is to observe, to "direct the eyes or mind, to set out and keep on course," then even though one may see conditioning and not always be free of it, there is still the possibility of observation having a greater and greater effect on what one sees as one's intention intensifies.

I
THE ESSENCE
of
LEARNING

OBSERVATIONS ON
PSYCHOLOGICAL CONDITIONING
&
AN EXAMINATION INTO THE
NATURE OF ENQUIRY AND INTELLIGENCE

In order to understand a new education, it is important to lay the foundation for this challenge. Before we can look at the new, having a clear understanding of what is happening now is a necessary prerequisite. Unless we do so, the new will become our ideal, another Utopian view, which will only breed more conflict because we are unable to attain what is desired.

In order to bring about a truly new education and a wholly different way of living, it is important to understand what *prevents* sane and intelligent living. The conventional approach to educational and social reform is through the positive, to invent some noble ideal to follow. But idealism, as we have explored in **Growing Up Sane**, cannot answer our psychological and social problems — it only creates more problems and further violence.

If the "positive approach" of idealism isn't the answer, what is? Can we see that idealism breeds conflict? If we do, then we are left with the *fact* of the violence caused by psychological conditioning. Psychological conditioning is the problem. The question is: "How do we approach solving this problem?" "How" implies a method, time, analysis, but, as noted previously, psychological conditioning must be observed in the present.

If we put aside the positive approach, then can we look directly at psychological conditioning as it is, not wanting to get rid of it but just to observe, to begin to see its structure, how it comes into being? Can we, through a process of elimination, put aside that which prevents understanding? Understanding what is *not* love or freedom, can we put aside our conditioning and, in so doing, bring about love, freedom? Putting aside conditioning means that we have understood it, have not only seen its superficial manifestations in society, but have traced it to its roots. By continually observing its nature, can we end it every time it arises, just by seeing conditioning for what it is? At first this seems difficult, but if one stays with it, it reveals itself more completely.

So, if we are serious about bringing about a new education, then we must look at the fact and not create another ideal. In order to understand the fact, two factors are involved: enquiry and intelligence. These factors are fundamental to a sane and intelligent life, and vital if we are to bring about a new education and hence a new child.

Again, we need to approach understanding through a process of elimination, finding out what is not intelligent. So what is enquiry? Or should we say, what is *not* enquiry. Enquiry is not a formula. It is not dogmatic assertion. Enquiry is not any fixed conclusion about life, nor is it an opinion to be forced on others. Enquiry is not, in other words, a psychological manipulation, a way of conditioning thought and behavior.

Without making enquiry into the ideal, can we see what it is? Enquiry is the capacity of insight, the ability to see into the nature of things, and to understand life as it is. Enquiry is a discovery from moment to moment, moving from insight to insight. In enquiry, the question arises, "What is the intelligent thing to do?"

Enquiry is philosophy in its purest form: the discovery of truth in everyday life. Philosophy has been formulated into ideals and beliefs by circuitous, convoluted thinking. Truth is understanding; truth is perception. Belief creates the illusion of what life *could* be. Truth, insight, intelligence, is understanding life as it is.

Enquiry is the movement of observation. Enquiry is not static. Enquiry is alive. It is the ability to see into things as they are. Enquiry does not create the illusion of ideals; it stays with the fact and, in so doing, understands it.

Thought is used as a means of conveying the insight that observation or enquiry has revealed. Thought is not the act of observation, of enquiry. It is only the vehicle for reflecting on and transmitting what was seen. Thought removed from observation, from insight, can create a maze of clever intellectual jargon to convince itself of its authority. This jargon creates the ideal of understanding. Understanding is not the ideal; it is learning in the present moment.

Although thought can — to some extent — understand itself, it is limited, time bound. Insight or
perception is not time bound and, therefore, can
end the reaction of conditioning as it arises in the
moment. Thinking about thinking may be the first
step in self-understanding, in becoming aware of
the nature and structure of thinking itself. But
there is always that gap, that space in time that
thinking creates, and because this level of understanding is not immediate, it can have no real
fundamental effect on conditioning.

The conventional approach to understanding is founded on tradition, conclusions, and fixed opinions about life. This convention is based on the intellectual capacity; that is, thought generating more thought. Perhaps at the beginning of the traditional approach there was a fundamental insight, but this soon deteriorated into belief as thought took over.

So, in order to enquire into the nature of psychological conditioning and how it affects behavior,
and to enquire into a new education for sane and
intelligent living, the mind cannot be caught in
opinion or in any conditioned conclusion about life.
This means that the mind is constantly learning,
not accumulating the past. The accumulation of
knowledge, as in science and technology, has a
place in living, but learning here means being
aware, watchful, observant, which is not accumulating information or knowledge.

Intelligence is another fundamental factor important to laying the foundation for understanding psychological conditioning in a new education. What is intelligence? What is the relationship of intelligence to knowledge?

How do we understand ourselves? What is the faculty that can understand psychological conditioning and conflict in relationship? We as teachers, parents and helping professionals have a responsibility to bring about this understanding in ourselves and our children.

The traditional approach to solving problems is through knowledge, through intellectual means. Therefore, the development of this faculty called "intelligence" is of primary importance to conventional educators. They have been concerned with finding out what it is in an attempt to systematically teach it to their students, developing numerous tests and activities with this in mind. And every parent wants his child to be "intelligent"; in that quest, parents endlessly read books and articles on the subject. To many parents, the development of intelligence involves their child's attendance at a good college and success therein, to secure economic survival.

In conventional education, intelligence is commonly equated with I.Q., the intellect, the ability to analyze abstract information. This ability does help us to solve technological and scientific challenges and has an important role to play in living, but this kind of problem solving capacity is mistakenly being applied to human relationship to improve psychological and social conditions. The intellect functions efficiently in the area of technology and science, but is it an appropriate tool for solving the problems of human relationship in the psychological and social realm?

The capacity to understand our lives psychologically and socially needs to be looked at *actually*, not intellectually. The intellect is thought, memory, which is the past. The problems of human relationship have traditionally been viewed through the intellect; that is, through thinking, through the past — hence, the imposition of tradition. The conventional approach to changing these problems has been to arrive at some solution, and then to apply the solution to the problem. Paradoxically, in the name of trying to bring about sane and healthy relationships, this process has created and sustained destructive behavior. This intellectual approach of trying to solve the psychological/ sociological problems of relationship through the intellect, commonly known as "intelligence," creates conflict because of the very structure of thinking itself, thinking requiring measurement in time.

Conflict comes about through thought measuring behavior in an attempt to change it.

Measurement, which is the nature of thought, creates a fundamental psychological conflict — the division between judgment of the quality that one wants to change and the ideal behavior one aspires to emulate.

The condemnation of certain behavior and the setting up of the ideal to follow is the habit of thought, because of its limited and specific function.

When one follows the ideal and negates the fact in order to change behavior, one is — by this very action — creating a conditioned state of reaction. That is, one's behavior becomes habitualized, directed toward an idealized, illusory goal. This is a rote, mechanical process.

By negating the undesirable behavior, one is creating a destructive process in wanting to eliminate that behavior. This process of trying to change behavior through thought or intellectual means is deeply ingrained in us. It not only creates psychological conflict, but also social conflict when the psychological is manifested outwardly. It is this fundamental conflict that needs to be examined: the way we approach solving the problems of relationship.

This process of trying to change behavior through intellectual means, through thought, is conditioning. This conditioning is perpetuated in society and most especially in our schools — overtly or as the "hidden curriculum" in the education of children. Education may be of the traditional academic kind or of a religious nature; in both, conditioning is the predominate factor.

This conditioning process has been justified as "socialization," a necessary process according to some "authorities" to bring about well-behaved, moral and "civilized" people. It is this conditioning process that needs to be explored so that the child may recognize it and not become its victim.

Since the word "intelligence" has come to mean the intellectual capacity and has been used inappropriately in trying to solve the problems of relationship, it is important to identify and cultivate the ability or capacity that *can* deal with psychological and social challenges. Unlike the intellect (thought, memory, the past), intelligence is the capacity to understand through immediate perception, without time, what is actually occurring in the moment. The faculty of intelligence is a heightened sense of observation. It is intelligence that will see through the conditioning process.

Intelligence is sensitivity to the living moment. It is this intelligence that uses the intellect when necessary, in its proper place. It is intelligence that understands the limits of thought and its destructive influence in the psychological realm.

The capacities of enquiry and intelligence are necessary for the truly educated human being. Enquiry stimulates the capacity of intelligence, which then has a life of its own.

We have created a highly skilled intellectual mind capable of great technological and scientific accomplishments, which has been instrumental in the development of our civilization. Now it is necessary to develop the capacity for insight, for it is this intelligence that will bring order to the intellect, to relationship, and to the world.

If intelligence is the capacity that understands conflict in relationship, then why haven't we been able to end such conflict? In other words, what has prevented intelligence from bringing about order in our lives? Again, perhaps we have approached the problem in the wrong way, trying to bring about intelligence through a process of positive reinforcement. Can we see the falseness of this process and how it, again, creates conflict? So then, what *is* the process of understanding, the process of intelligence? By understanding what *prevents* order, can we bring about order?

By understanding what is not intelligent, can we bring about intelligence? By a process of elimination, can we arrive at the positive? Is this the "how," the direction to look anew? Or is this just too simple?

Where do we go from here? Are we still waiting to learn "how" to understand psychological conditioning? Are we so conditioned by being told what to do that we cannot find out for ourselves?

II
A
NEW EDUCATION
for
SANE AND INTELLIGENT
LIVING

THE INTENTION OF A NEW SCHOOL
&
A PRESENTATION OF A NEW PERSPECTIVE
IN TEACHING ACADEMICS
AND LIVING SKILLS

We have discussed psychological conditioning, its danger individually and socially, and the need for understanding. In essence, we have been looking at ourselves, how we have been reared and how we, in turn, are rearing our children. Can we now suspend our conventional views of education and child rearing to look from a new perspective? Can we now begin our enquiry, having examined our past, into the possibilities for a brave *new* child, a young person who is being helped to understand and be free from psychological conditioning and the conditioning influences in society? Can we see what this new child might be like — without creating more ideals to impose?

In understanding this brave *new* child, we will need to look at the educational environment that would encourage an unconditional perspective, a perspective that sees life as it is. Perhaps we need to start with the intention of such a school, looking at the conditions that foster intelligent growth. What would some of the basic intentions be of this new education?

Perhaps the most important intention of a school is to provide an environment that is free from fear. Fear prevents real learning and needs to be addressed within the school and at home — and not just at the level of the many fears we have, but at the root of fear itself, the fundamental fear for psychological survival. It is fear that is the primary cause of violence and must be understood if we are to live sane and intelligent lives. Unfortunately, most approaches to eliminating fear are based on fear and only compound the problem.

In this school, a child will be encouraged to understand what love is. In order to understand love, the student will come to understand that sentiment and emotionalism can be destructive and are not love. For instance, the playing of national anthems and the political frenzy generated by emotional displays of patriotism are forces that can destroy the quality of love. Love will be enquired into, to see how conditional it has become. Such questions may arise in this enquiry as: "Is love romantic?" "Is love personal?" or "Is love that quality of intelligence that is beyond the personal, beyond the isolation of self-centeredness?"

Another intention will be to help each young person find out what he cares to do in life. So often, children are influenced to follow what they and others think they should do. Hence, they lose the sense of what they really care about, their natural inclination. This does not mean that they are encouraged to be selfish. Finding out what one cares to do is not selfishness. It is intelligence.

An intelligent educational environment will not condition the child to be successful, to become someone important, to want power. Such a school will not foster isolating, self-centered activities that create conventional desires for fame, wealth or status. This school will help the child understand why such desires come about, why traditional education has emphasized the individual, the divided and fragmented human being. Without understanding, the child would be vulnerable to the tremendous pressures of society to be a part of the mainstream of convention.

This school would encourage the understanding of conflict, both internally and externally. Outwardly, the child needs to look at war, mankind's brutal manifestation of inward conflict. The child would not be encouraged to enter into external conflict, i.e., to join the armed forces, but rather to find healthy, nonviolent alternatives to hostility. The child will be encouraged to go deeply into this issue of conflict to see if he can understand the problem at the root. It is under-standing conflict, fundamentally, that will bring about resolution of the manifestations of conflict.

The child will also need to understand nationalism and patriotism, to see the danger of identifying with a political fragment, of upholding a particular cultural perspective. The school will not encourage adulation of heroes or patriots because of the divisive nature of such sentiment.

The school will help the young person question established religious practices and to enquire into the nature of belief systems. The child will be encouraged to develop the qualities of the religious mind, a mind free of psychological conditioning.

The child will need to look at his relationship to the family, and between his family and other families. He will enquire into the nature of healthy relationships and will be encouraged to embrace the family of mankind, rather than focusing identity on that which is isolating and fragmentary.

In the community, the child needs to become aware of potentially destructive influences and the various fragmentary groups and organizations that create conflict in relationship through the creation of false allegiance in their quest for psychological identification.

Another concern of an intelligent school will be to help the student understand the business world, right livelihood, and a "healthy" relationship to money — not to be seduced by senseless, endless profit. In this society, the child is often encouraged to be greedy and to justify this greed as "good" enterprise. Understanding the right relationship to money can aid in understanding fear and competition.

Understanding the influence of the media is vital to an intelligent education. Being conscious of the influence of advertising, of programming that is unhealthy, is of utmost importance since media has such a tremendous effect on the brain.

Helping the child know what being a parent means is essential to growing up intelligently. Parenting skills of bearing and caring for children are rarely taught to young people. It is important for young people to understand the institution of marriage, how conditioned we are in our expectations of marriage, and what an intelligent relationship to one's partner and children is, so they are able to respond sanely to the challenges of family life.

Exploration of what it means to be a man or a woman is also part of an intelligent education. This is where conditioning becomes quite evident. The traditional man's role requires the facade of being tough, strong, calm, unemotional, in control, brave. Whereas a woman's role is conventionally seen as all embracing, forgiving, emotional, sacrificing, fragile, and so on. These myths that we have been conditioned to believe must be examined so the young person can be free to live as a whole human being, expressing the qualities of both femininity and masculinity.

Intelligent and caring educators will encourage respect for all life. We need to explore the uncaring use of animals for our own pleasure, and the barbaric act of killing for food, sport, or fashion.

The child will be encouraged to understand the natural world, and to develop patience and care by attending to growing food. Caring for an organic garden and becoming sensitive to the cycles of nature contribute to a proper understanding of growth, harmony, and healthful living. The student learns patience, balance and order when nature is the teacher.

The teaching of academics in such an educational environment would help young people understand vital issues and the implications of psychological conditioning, instead of being a means by which they are conditioned. For the most part, academics have traditionally been learned through the slow and painfully tedious memorization of facts and figures. This is not to deny that fine teachers and schools have taken care and time to teach academics intelligently and passionately but, unfortunately, they are the minority.

The teaching of history can become an adventure into the nature of relationship, enlightening students in how the mind selectively re-creates the past and uses that knowledge to influence behavior in the present. If the teacher is aware of the need to understand the fundamental cause of the problems of relationship, then a subject like history can become a mirror in which a child can see himself. History has traditionally been taught so that we can learn from our mistakes. Can we challenge the notion that we learn from our past mistakes? Can we show the child that history is biased according to the particular culturally conditioned perspective of the historian? Can we see that history has been a means of conditioning young minds to believe in a particular way, thereby creating fragmentation (my history versus your history; my country versus your country) which perpetuates global conflict?

Learning languages can be a way for the young person to understand conditioning and fear. Apprehension of something or someone "foreign" is commonplace, especially if that something or someone is from a culture one has been particularly conditioned against — Germany and German, for instance. Films about the Second World War created such fear of this culture that there was a time when we imagined every German to be a Nazi. And we had the same emotional response to the Japanese. Today, Russia and China produce that reaction. When a child learns a language, or learns to say a few words in many languages, those images of fear, of the foreigner, are broken. The child begins to see that people are people, despite the superficial differences of language and custom. This is so simple a task with such important implications that one wonders why it isn't undertaken everywhere, in all schools. An intelligently planned school would teach some basic, simple everyday expressions in many languages, thereby helping to break the barriers of ignorance and prejudice.

The school fostering intelligence would teach science humanely, with a deep sense of caring. No intelligent human being would want to invent destructive weapons. A sensitive person would not be able to torture animals experimentally. Science should be taught with great compassion, always considering its ethical implications.

Traditional subjects such as psychology, anthropology, sociology, economics and business can be taught intelligently if there is a fundamental understanding of how conflict arises in relationship. If that understanding is absent, life is viewed from self-centered isolated fear and the student is taught that "I" — over all others — must survive, that "I" must succeed and be someone. Academic subjects can enhance the quality of life only when personal interests are not the primary concern. With intelligence, these pursuits help us blossom; with ignorance, they turn against us, creating pollution, waste and destruction.

Some subjects, such as the arts, can enlighten the student about aspects of human behavior. The arts allow the child to stay in contact with the wonder of life beyond the word, that essence of livingness that is the foundation of all life.

The child also needs to understand his body, how to exercise correctly and eat nutritionally sound foods. This does not imply that the traditional view of a balanced diet is appropriate. On the contrary, this requires the questioning of that conventional view, looking at ethical questions related to our diet such as the eating of meat, the humane treatment of animals, and health and ecological issues. A healthy body is the foundation for well-being. This is nothing new, but to change our ways of approaching and maintaining well-being, to see beyond our conditioned views about a healthy lifestyle, will require deep introspection. What better place to start than early in the life of the child.

Manners and etiquette are attributes that an intelligent school would encourage in the child. This may sound old-fashioned, but it is important for young people to be able to dress, eat and speak appropriately according to the occasion. A host of other social relationship skills are also necessary for ease of cooperation among people. In the past, such skills were taught punitively and children often rebelled at such training. However, this awareness can be taught with affection, sensitivity and appropriateness.

Communication skills such as being able to creatively handle disagreements, everyday conflicts, and the parent/child relationship; understanding how to cope with sibling rivalry and family life; and making and keeping friends are all important parts of creating a healthy life. Understanding how to make intelligent decisions, solve problems creatively, cope with danger, watch television intelligently, manage time and money, and deal with consumerism are requirements of a child's life today that need to be taught at the individual level.

Helping the child understand trauma is essential to reducing anxiety. Separation, divorce, moving, adding a new person to the family, nightmares, visits to the doctor, dentist or hospital, injuries, death, handicaps, and adoption are potentially traumatic events that a child may need to face. Wonderful self-help books for children are available on these subjects and can be used at home or in the classroom; they are a necessary and vital part of any school.

There are also some largely overlooked everyday skills a child needs to learn, such as cleaning his room. This may seem simple to us, but it can be an organizational nightmare for some young people.

Perhaps the reason we do not generally teach these skills is because many of us have conditioned views about children. Many adults see children as cute, helpless, cuddly creatures incapable of any intelligent reasoning ability. This is exemplified by the children's books that are best sellers, stories about cute bunny rabbits and bears and a fantasy land of adorable forest friends. Most people think that a child should be a child as long as possible — then at some magical point, usually in adolescence, they should suddenly become adults. Perhaps because many adults are caught up in endless routine, boring jobs they don't like, marriages full of conflict, and lives that are generally unhappy and meaningless, childhood seems a happy, innocent time of play without responsibilities. But they are mistaken: children daily face the same challenges as adults but with little or no experience in how to handle them. Children experience trauma and are deeply and lastingly affected. Innocence does not help; it hinders understanding. Every day, children must negotiate difficulties, ranging from organizational matters such as cleaning their rooms to psychosocial matters such as disputes with brothers, sisters or friends.

Children are not exempt from the hurts and difficulties of daily life. They need to be able to meet these challenges intelligently, and they need to be taught how to do so. Children learn most social skills through a tremendous number of trial and error frustrations. There is a place for trial and error — it is a good teacher — but learning living skills can be crucial to a child. Every school can teach these skills within the normal span of time the child is in the classroom.

III
EDUCATION
&
SELF-DISCOVERY

ENQUIRING INTO
THE STRUCTURE OF CONSCIOUSNESS
&
THE ROOTS OF LEARNING

Let us go deeper in our enquiry than academic learning and living skills, into the very core of learning, to understand not only the content of thinking but also its nature and structure. Consciousness, or thinking, forms our behavior and shapes our relationship to the world. If we are to bring about a new education, a new child and a new way of living, then we must examine this fundamental process, for in our thinking lies the source of conflict. Educational reform is not enough. Pushing the child into more and more intellectual activities evades the central issue. Educating a child requires an entirely new perspective, a view that will enable him to see the problem of conflict in its entirety, the root as well as its manifestation.

We have begun to create a foundation for a healthy educational environment by understanding the role of knowledge in learning and living. Now, can there be a more profound learning that opens a child's mind to view the fundamental causes of conflict, a means to awakening the process of self-discovery within the child?

The intent of an intelligent education is to help a child discover the fundamental source of conflict. By creating activities that mirror his state of mind, one can give the student insight into the structure and nature of thinking. Such activities would become the core of the school's curriculum, because teachers would understand the vital need to explore the actual movement of consciousness in action in daily life. The teachers of this school will feel the urgency of this challenge, knowing the importance of having a comprehensive understanding of the rudiments of conflict and how the brain operates. Teachers will need to demonstrate the nature and structure simply so a student can comprehend the basic formation of his own thinking instrument. In other words, teachers will introduce the young person to himself, to the workings of the human brain, simply and directly, knowing that this self-introduction will enable the student to begin to grasp the basic operations of mental activity and human behavior, and the workings of psychological conditioning. Such an endeavor will be the foundation of a new education.

In order to begin to grasp the structure of psychological conditioning and conflict, the child will be encouraged to look at the brain, the seat of thinking and emotions, in an objective, mechanical way. What is perceived needs to be looked at scientifically, without emotional judgment or condemnation. The child will be encouraged to allow the psychological self to come into the view and scrutiny of objective, scientific observation. The student will be encouraged to freely but nonjudgmentally explore the content, as well as the structure, of his consciousness. In this way the child will begin to understand the basic operation of (his) thinking — intellectual as well as psychological.

In this new education, the child will be encouraged not to separate, divide or categorize what he sees. Traditionally, when studying the mind, we have judged or analyzed the content of consciousness, dividing it into separate parts: conscious, subconscious, and unconscious. In this new school, one would experience consciousness as a whole, ever changing, undivided process.

In this new education, the child will be encouraged to let what has conventionally been categorized and repressed as the subconscious or unconscious to come into the light of awareness so that there is an understanding of what is lying beneath our everyday conscious awareness. Therefore, in the bringing together of seemingly separate parts, there is an ending of a fundamental division.

When we believe in the division of conscious, subconscious, and unconscious, there is a need to repress one part in favor of another. This need to suppress or control subconscious or unconscious thoughts, emotions and urges creates the "controller," or the thinker, controlling thoughts. As we explored in **Growing Up Sane**, this thinker controlling thoughts is at the root of disorder and needs to be approached with care in the process of discovering the fundamental causes of psychological conflict.

This new school will need to prepare the child adequately for viewing the flow of unconscious thoughts, feelings and urges. It will be very important not to judge what one sees, just to let that which is being viewed pass into awareness, and out again, and be done with it. The child can also be shown how awareness becomes identified with mental content, creating the illusion that thoughts are a continuous, unbroken reality, not just separate passing elements in an endless succession of fragmented thinking. Consciousness or awareness, through identification, therefore, can become constricted to a fixed viewpoint.

At first, the flow of unrestricted, unconscious thinking may seem frightening to the young person, for it may appear that the dreaming world has entered the waking world, that nightmares have come into the daylight. An intelligent parent or teacher can assure the child that these thoughts, images, feelings and urges are like a dream, that he does not have to act on them. This is *very* important for the child to see. He does not want to identify with what comes up. It is important to ask the child to view these thoughts and images as if watching a movie, and at the same time to be aware that he is not actually in the movie but that he is, rather, a nonjudgmental observer.

This new school would not only encourage the content of consciousness to flow undivided and unimpeded, but would also encourage the child to explore the nature and structure of consciousness. For centuries humankind has analyzed the content of consciousness. In understanding the roots of conflict, we are not as interested in the analysis of content as in allowing the content to be viewed without the controlling and divisive aspect of the thinker separate from thoughts.

Beginning to understand the structure of consciousness, of thinking, means that the child becomes aware of the mechanical nature of thought. The child begins to see how thinking operates, as if he were studying the internal-combustion engine. The child begins to understand how conditioning comes into being, what causes it, and how it works.

As the child begins to allow the unimpeded flow of the content of consciousness to happen, and begins to discover the mechanical repetitive structure of thinking and the restrictions inherent in psychological attachment, he enters a fundamental process of learning, of discovering himself. It is this process of discovery that is intelligence, the capacity to be aware, sensitive and alert. Intelligence is a self-perpetuating light; it grows stronger as one sees more clearly. Intelligence brings about intelligence, and one is able to move from insight to insight.

This new school will provide a direction for the child to look, to enquire into. The school can prepare the child for this journey into self-discovery by helping him to understand and proceed without fear into his own psyche and brain, which is the human brain. And in so doing, the young person opens the door to endless wonder, a new frontier in discovery.

Can we *really* help the child to fundamentally understand the nature and structure of thinking, to see where thinking as an instrument of measurement has a place in living and where it causes conflict? Now we educate the child by filling up his consciousness with technological and scientific information. Can we also see that we educate the child to fill up his consciousness with information of a psychological nature? What does it mean to create a consciousness of "psychological information"? What is this psychological information? What need does it fulfill? How do we deal with this information of psychological content?

Can we help the child begin to see that the content of psychological information is the past: collectively, our historical past; individually, what comprises "me"? Can we help the child see that this psychological content is divisive (you/me, he/she, we/they, American/Russian, Arab/Israeli) and therefore a source of conflict inwardly and outwardly? The Arab says that his land comes from his forefathers; the Israeli says the same. Each is identified with the content — the psychological history — each has as his own conditioned perspective, and therefore there is perpetual violence.

If we see the danger of this psychological content, this collection of information that is "me," what can we help the child do about it? Within oneself, who or what is the entity that is going to do something about it? If the psychological content of consciousness is "me," "I," can I do something about myself?

Can we help the child realize that "I" cannot "do" anything about the content? Can we help the child see that "doing" something implies that "I" is separate from the content, that the "I" is somehow different from the "me" and can therefore act upon itself? Or are we just playing with words here, playing with our psychological well-being?

Is it possible to see that psychological "problems" cannot be "solved"? Is it possible to show children that there is nothing one can "do" about the conflict thoughts produce? Conflict arises when we try to end psychological problems through effort, through analysis, through trying to "solve" the problems of psychological conflict. Is it possible for the brain to deeply forget, to see the futility of action to end psychological problems? What happens when we come to this realization? Where is our awareness now? What is the faculty that has come upon this realization, that has understood the truth or falseness of what has been written here? Is this intelligence?

It is possible that an intelligent teacher can show children in simple ways how the structure and nature of thought works. One activity a child can participate in is to watch his own mind. For instance, ask the children to see in their "mind's eye" a favorite place, food, or person. Ask them to watch what happens. Are they aware of any feelings associated with their mental images? Where do these images and feelings come from? Then ask them to imagine their least favorite person, place, or food. Where do these images and feelings come from? Are they aware of how these images and feelings affect their behavior? Then ask them to remember an argument they had in the past, and to review the argument as best as possible, to get back into that feeling state. Can they solve this past argument? Finally, ask them to forget images and feelings and be aware of the present moment, to just look and listen without judging what is occurring. Let them sit there for awhile and allow this to happen. Then ask them what happened to the argument and their feelings about whoever they were arguing with, and the negative thoughts and feelings they had before.

Helping the child to understand the nature and structure of thinking, of consciousness, gives him a more profound understanding of the problems of relationship and the causes of psychological conflict. Do we see the importance of this? In Part IV we will look at some practical ways we can demonstrate this understanding.

IV
A SAMPLE CURRICULUM
for
UNDERSTANDING
PSYCHOLOGICAL CONDITIONING

(**Note**: Presented here are sample exercises or activities that can aid teachers and parents in helping children understand psychological conditioning. My intention is to stimulate teachers and parents to find other ways to demonstrate this theme to children, based on their own observation. In this way, everyone involved enters into the problem with intelligence, with the intention to find out for themselves.)

In keeping with the core intention of a *new* school for the *brave new child,* one that helps students understand psychological conditioning and go beyond it, it is vital that we develop a practical curriculum that exposes children to the nature and structure of psychological conditioning. Such a curriculum is not a methodology, or form of conditioning children to be unconditioned; rather, it provides a mirror so that the child can see the workings of his own mind, and thus perceive the foundation of psychological conditioning.

This perception can be achieved simply in a variety of ways. For example, show the child a model of the brain that represents mechanically how thought works. Either a diagram or working movable model of the brain can demonstrate the similarity of the structure of thought to the functioning of a movie projector. The model should show the mechanical aspects of thinking and how information may be stored and projected, including both factual information about the world and the psychological information that we accept as "me." This psychological information will appear as projected prejudices that color what we see, think, or feel.

Take a child on a blindfold walk, or let another child or adult guide him around a safe area. [I have personally done this many times with children.] Have the child touch many different objects, the last being water. Invariably the blindfolded child will be surprised as he or she touches water. Now take the blindfold off and let the child go through the same sequence of touching things. When he puts his hand into water the second time, he is usually not surprised. Sit down and discuss the difference between the two occasions of touching water. Why did he act so surprised when he touched water the first time while blindfolded, and why wasn't he surprised when he could see what he was doing? Children usually say that they were surprised the first time because they didn't *know* that it was water, but the second time they *knew* what it was. Then discuss the difference between the two experiences to discover how knowledge works: when the brain knows about water, that knowledge eliminates the element of surprise *of contacting the essence of water in the moment as if for the first time.* The second time the child touches water, he knows what it will feel like; he contacts water through the filter of the past, with familiarity and an element of boredom.

[Prejudgment separates us from direct experience of the present moment by setting comparative standards to evaluate experience. This comparative prejudging distorts reality and can cause conflict in the psychological realm between what actually is and what should or should not be.

Technologically or scientifically, comparison, of course, is a necessary process for innovation.]

We then talk with the children about other psychological situations in which the mind prejudges, and how prejudice affects the quality of living and relationship. For example, do we look at our friends or family with prejudgment, holding on to past images of hurt or anger that cloud perception? One can observe how the brain, by storing past information and re-projecting it, taints the present moment. We talk about how this prejudging affects not only ourselves but also the global situation. In other words, starting from a simple perception of how the brain functions, we can see how that way of functioning affects the whole of society. We then see that the individual problem is the same as the social problem; the fundamental capacity to prejudge is both individual and collective. In other words, the conflict in oneself and in the world are one and the same.

*

Show a geographical map of the world to children and ask them to tell you what they see. When I did this, the children said they saw oceans, mountains, rivers, continents, and the like. Then show them a political map of the world and ask them what they see. In my case, they said they saw countries, nations, cities, and so on. When I asked them about the differences between the two maps, they said that the geographical map was not

"broken up" and that the political map was
"broken up into pieces." Then we discussed how
the geographical map became the political map.
My students said that thought created division and
fragmentation into nations, and broke up the
whole. I then asked them how we might restore
the whole and they talked about the United
Nations. We discussed how the "United Nations" is
an "oxymoron," a contradiction in terms, and the
impossibility of creating wholeness out of fragmentation. We talked about how representatives from
nations cannot bring about world peace and
cooperation if they continue to identify with their
particular fragment. They felt that if the individuals
which make up the United Nations would see the
truth of this rather simple fact, they could drop
their identity and, in so doing, there would can be
wholeness, cooperation. And until this happens,
there is inherent conflict. The harder the delegates
try to bring about cooperation or order, the more
disorder is created. Arabs continue to kill Israelis,
Iranians continue to war with Iraqis, as humans
have done for thousands of years.

*

Many simple experiments can demonstrate or
mirror to children how thought works. But perhaps
we need to prepare the child's mind for this more
sophisticated awareness of the thinking process
with some preliminary exercises in perception.
When children are able to observe the subtle
nuances of the ordinary around them, they can

then move on to more complex observations, such as observing a thought or emotion: we start with the simple and ordinary and move out from there.

Let me share with you an example of how a teacher or parent can enhance a child's awareness — for it is a heightened sense of *awareness* that is necessary to perceive the subtle movements of one's mind, the subtle fluctuations of conditioning and the fixed conclusions one has about living.

Try a simple writing assignment: ask the students to describe an ordinary object — for example, a simple kitchen match. At first, young people usually see very little when asked to look. They may write, "A match is wooden and has a red tip that lights." This is limited perception. What stands in the way of enhanced perception (as is shown in the description that follows) is one's *image* that a "match" is just an ordinary thing, something not worth one's time. It is this prejudice, this prejudgment, that causes the narrowing and limiting of one's world. What is necessary is to first observe that we are doing this, to actually see that we are conditioned to regard the ordinary as "ordinary." Then, we can begin to look at life with more care, with increased awareness and enhanced sensitivity, to see the ordinary as extraordinary.

Here is a wonderful example of enhanced awareness from the book, <u>Here and Now</u>, by Fred Morgan (reprinted with permission of publisher*):

THE MATCH

"The kitchen match I have in my hand is a stick of light-colored wood about two and one-half inches long and an eighth of an inch thick. The wood is soft and has been finished roughly so that small slivers curl up from the surfaces and corners here and there.

"About one-fourth of an inch at one end of the stick has been pinched — as though some sort of machine had been used to grip it — in such a way that the corners are flattened, making the end of the stick nearly round. At the other end of the stick, a lump of red grainy material is attached. This lump is shaped much like an avocado, with the end of the stick thrust into the stem end of the fruit. The lump is only slightly larger in diameter than the stick. The edges of the lump which overlap the stick have an uneven, flowing appearance, as though the grainy solid had once been a liquid into which the stick was dipped. The last sixteenth of an inch of this lump, the part which would be the blossom end of the avocado, consists of a white cap of material similar to the rest of the lump except for its color. When examined closely, the surfaces of both the red and the white parts

*Fred Morgan, <u>Here and Now</u> (New York: Harcourt Brace Jovanovich, Publishers, 1968), pp. 8-10.

are seen to sparkle with minute, glittering grains like fine sand.

"The wood of the stick smells like fir or spruce. It has a slightly unnatural taste, as though it had been chemically treated. The lump at the end is heavier than the wood, so that when the stick is dropped it falls lump first and hits with the white cap down. The lump seems to have no distinct taste; however, when it is dampened, it emits an acid smell. When the stick falls on a hard surface, the sound of contact is a sharp "clink," almost musical, indicating that the wood is dry in spite of its softness. When the stick is broken between the fingers, the sharp snap it makes confirms this. In addition, it breaks in such a biased way as to indicate that the length of the stick does not exactly correspond with the grain of the wood.

"When the white cap is scratched vigorously against a rough surface, it suddenly bursts into nearly white flame with a loud crack. Immediately the white cap turns black and ignites the red portion of the lump, which burns rapidly back toward the stick with a large yellow flame, hissing and smoking slightly with a strong, acrid smell. The burning of the red portion is less vigorous than that of the white, but strong enough to force tongues of flame outward and downward as well as upward. It is consumed in about two seconds, during which the stick itself is ignited. The lump is now entirely black and somewhat larger than before, and the flame reduces itself from a flaring burst about two inches high to a steady triangle about an inch high as it travels slowly along the length of the stick, pushing ahead of it a ring of clear liquid which seems to sweat out of the wood. The triangle is bright yellow flame except at the base, where it is transparent, and along the bottom beneath the stick, where it is a distinct blue color. Occasionally the apex of the triangle wavers and extends itself upward into a long thread of darker orange flame which becomes a thin streamer of black smoke. The only sound at this time is an intermittent crackling together with a very faint hissing or boiling sound. The acrid smell has been replaced by the smell of burning wood.

"As the flame moves back along it, the stick first browns, then blackens, glows bright red, shrinks to half its original thickness, curls, and finally blackens again, emitting a stream of white smoke. In its final form, after the flame has passed, the stick is black, shiny, and curled upward with small wrinkles or bumps along its top edge, and it has become so brittle that it easily crumbles into black powder when it is touched. If it is handled carefully, the swollen head of harder black material will remain attached, and the entire object will be a shrunken and twisted replica of what it was before the burning. If it is dropped gently from an inch or so onto a hard surface, it will make a brittle, high-pitched metallic sound, and if it is broken it will snap off quickly and cleanly. Its smell now is the familiar smell of wood ashes. If the head is crumbled carefully and the texture of the different parts observed, it can be discovered that the stick originally extended through the lump of red grainy material to the base of the white cap."

Can you see how that writer's perception has come alive? Usually one looks at ordinary objects but never really sees! It is this "seeing" or awareness that needs to be awakened in us if we are to understand the complexities of our conditioned thinking.

If the intention of a new school is to help the child understand psychological conditioning, then it is vital that the teachers demonstrate it directly. The child needs to intellectually understand, for example, the process of projection and identification if he is to begin to have a deeper understanding of how thought works, how thought conditions behavior and forms the "me," and all the conflict which that produces. As educators, we need to explore with the child the whole of thinking, the technological *and* the psychological realms, and to help the child question the proper place of thought in living. If we do not, then that child will be lopsided — intellectually capable but psychologically unaware.

V
THE MARTIAL ARTS
in
EDUCATION

SOLVING CONFLICT NONVIOLENTLY:
A Look at How the Practice
of Martial Arts Can Help People
Avoid Reacting Physically to
Psychological Threats

This section deals with violence, and with helping children learn how to cope with this aspect of life in creative ways. My childhood was fraught with violence, growing up just outside New York City in the 1940's and 1950's. I feel that teaching young people how to get out of potentially violent situations is just as important as teaching them intellectual or other living skills. The world at large is a terribly violent place, and young people need to learn how to live peaceably in this time of great conflict.

The Martial Arts have a terrible public image. When most people hear the word "Karate," they think of violent war movies in which this skill is used to kill or maim the enemy. Paradoxically, Karate — an endeavor I have been involved with for nearly thirty years — is a way to gentleness and nonviolence, *if it is taught intelligently.*

Traditionally, the Martial Arts — especially Karate — have been conceived of as military endeavors, teaching that the honorable solution to the problems of relationship is through violence and combat. Whenever I go into a school to talk with children, I find that they have been exposed to this culturally heroic ideal of fighting as a solution to conflict. The media has exploited and glorified this attitude. I am concerned that our children, already conditioned in this way, be exposed to another, more humane, view. A powerful and effective nonviolent discipline is available through the Martial Arts, the very tool that has often promoted violence.

The Martial Arts are excellent vehicles for physical fitness; they are fun and exciting sports which do not have to be overly competitive. More importantly, the Martial Arts as self-defense are a way to dispel harmful aggression ethically and effectively by developing a person's confidence to neutralize hostility by alternative, nonviolent means. (It has also been demonstrated that, as a by-product of Karate training, a child's learning process is greatly enhanced by this unique type of physical movement; children taking Karate have shown a greater aptitude for scholastic endeavors.)

In our Karate classes, we help children study self-defense skills to develop the confidence *not* to fight. By using role-playing techniques, we teach them to avoid potential conflict by using non-threatening alternatives. Some of these creative alternatives are: making friends, humor, trickery, walking away, refusing to fight, reasoning it out, calling the proper authority, and so on. The point, which is actually quite simple, is to have the confidence to step back from fear, to create a gap, a distance from the primitive fight-or-flight mechanism that is our instinctive survival reaction. When fear is in a state of abeyance, one's mind is free to find intelligent alternatives to the situation. The key is to create this gap, to abate fear, so one can respond to the specific situation at hand instead of reacting blindly. *Respond* means to act with intelligence; *react* means to *re-act*, to act in a habitual, generally fearful manner. Sometimes to react with our fight-or-flight mechanism is appropriate; for example, when a car is about to run over us or our house is on fire, there is an advantage in instant unthinking reaction. But what we are talking about here are alternatives to a violent reaction in a conflict situation.

The issue of conflict is complex. We need to look beyond the surface symptoms to understand the underlying causes of conflict and violence in relationship. I am offering a way in which we can look at violence directly, nonjudgmentally, by using the Martial Art of Karate as a context for that observation. I think that it is important to ask some fundamental questions about conflict, questions such as, "What is fear?" and "How does fear come about?" For I see fear as an underlying factor in conflict, both individually and socially.

Let's go step by step into this question of fear, conflict and violence. How does fear affect our lives? Why and when do we feel anxiety? In what ways do we pass on our fears to our children? How are we presently solving the problem of fear? Can a Martial Art such as Karate help us to understand and cope with fear, conflict and violence? Perhaps we can start by looking at the general situation first, then work towards the particular.

Why are we often in a state of reaction psychologically, a continual, inappropriate state of feeling that we are threatened, that our survival is constantly in danger? We are continually being bombarded by images of violence — on television, in magazines, newspapers, and movies. The media presents the world as a terrible, threatening and violent place, in which seemingly every dark alley, every unlit parking lot, every home at night is inviting danger. The constant exposure to images of violence takes its toll on us. We are afraid! We used to be able to go out at night and not feel anxious; now we are constantly worried about what might happen to us, whether we will be attacked, mugged, raped or murdered! And hanging over us all is the fear of "the enemy," the fear that we will be annihilated by nuclear weapons. It's not just a local conflict; the whole world is jeopardized. It's not just the "other" who is being threatened, it is also "me," "I," who is threatened — and it appears to be getting worse!

Now, what does this constant exposure to images of violence do to us? What effect do these images have on our behavior? When we face an actual threat, we react in a "fight-or-flight" manner. This fight-or-flight mechanism, located deep in the layers of the old brain, protects us from injury by sending messages to those parts of the brain responsible for handling self-protective action. It also sends a powerful hormone, adrenaline, which gives the body a quick burst of energy to carry out its survival tactics. Fight-or-flight is a healthy brain function that is sometimes needed to protect the body from physical harm.

The images in the media are only images. But we seem to mistake images for the real thing since the old brain fight-or-flight response does not differentiate between a psychological and physical threat. It just reacts to "threat," which triggers a self-protective reaction by sending powerful hormones to stimulate the body to quick action, either by attacking or fleeing the situation.

Now the problem compounds itself. These *images* of violence constantly remind us of the "real" world (the world we created by our images — a self-fulfilling prophecy) so that we are constantly being stimulated to react *as if* there are *actual* threats to our immediate physical survival.

It appears to me that we have become locked into a fight-or-flight reaction, that our tremendous energy to be aggressive derives, in part, from being constantly stimulated by this mechanism. It is as though the mechanism has become fused, locked in the "on" position, and we are living out a continual adrenaline rush.

So, since we see our world as being under constant threat, we want to end that threat — a logical deduction if we want to live sanely. But how do we go about it? Perhaps because we do not see the real cause of the problem, we act superficially to create temporary solutions. We want our children to be able to deal effectively with "the threat," and we perceive it as being inside, outside, or both. Generally, people see an outside agent as the enemy. To the Americans, "it" is the Russians. To the Russians, "it" is the Americans. So we teach our children to be prepared to meet the enemy defensively. And we militarize.

Another outside threat that we perceive is economic, the persistent precariousness of our financial well-being. We see other people as competitors against whom we need to wage "war" in business. We promote our products aggressively, afraid that competitors will get to market first. We pressure our children to get high grades, enter good colleges, and land high-paying prestigious jobs.

We also perceive an "internal enemy," that some religious people label as the "Devil," which must be exorcised through moral education. To various degrees, many people feel this to be true; for instance, one religion states, and its congregation believes, that children are born in original sin. We have talked about this and the contradiction of trying to bring about goodness through ideals in **Growing Up Sane**. Perhaps here we can look at the problem in another light and see the terrible pressure we are putting on our children in order to meet the "internal enemy."

It is as though we are biologically driven to be violent, to react to the world as a totally threatening place, to drive ourselves and our children to defend, to insanely compete. And our usual solutions to these problems cause more pressure and violence.

Perhaps we can deal with the problem in a more intelligent way. As a working hypothesis, let's say that we have mistaken *images* of violence or psychological threat as real imminent danger to physical survival and, in so doing, have stimulated the fight-or-flight mechanism into a state of continual alert. We have tried to deal with the threat conventionally, assuming that it is real and reacting with military defense, competition or moralizing. Now, if we observe our own actions, we can perhaps see what we can do to end the problem fundamentally, at its root. If the fight-or-flight mechanism has become locked or fused into a constant state of reaction to threat, then it makes sense to defuse that mechanism. In other words, we need to create a gap so that this pattern of instinctive reaction is broken.

What can create this "gap" in the fused fight-or-flight mechanism? The old brain reaction to a physical threat needs to be reeducated and the confidence gained that we can cope with the threat of aggression. For a simple example on the individual level: if a young person is being threatened by another child, the brain registers, "Here is a threat. Can I defend myself?" If the young person has been trained to defend himself (by Karate, for example), then the answer is "Yes," and a gap is created, forestalling the fight-or-flight reaction. In other words, the fight/flight mechanism is not immediately triggered; it is "inhibited" which prevents the "firing" of the signal to arouse this reaction. During this gap, pause, or "inhibited state," fear is temporarily suspended and the young person has the opportunity to respond intelligently, especially if he or she has been shown nonviolent alternatives (as in Take Nami Do Karate). If the child has not been trained to defend himself, then a self-protective reaction to the threat may occur and, thus, the problem begins.

But breaking this automatic reaction by learning self-defense techniques and nonviolent alternatives is only a temporary measure. There may be no need to react with the survival mechanism if we give the old brain the confidence that it can defend itself, but we are only touching the surface; this is the starting point for a deeper enquiry into the source of the problem and the social structures created by our conditioned reaction to threat. The continual, habitual reaction to a threat is caused by conditioning; if we are to break the habit, we have to see our response for what it is. Observing conditioning will initiate its own action. In order for us to free ourselves of a conditioned reaction, we must observe its structure, and then we may see that the brain has misinterpreted a psychological threat for a physical threat and is unnecessarily primed to react defensively.

If what has been said here is recognized as

true, because we have looked at it for ourselves, then we have a grasp of the basic problems of fear, conflict and violence. If serious interest has been stimulated, then we can move deeper into these fundamental issues.

The practice of the Art of Karate offers a creative context within which to explore alternative methods of coping with violence. The intelligent practice of the Martial Arts is a vehicle for understanding ourselves, which is the ultimate goal of education.

VI
OBSERVATIONS
on
EDUCATION AND LIVING

COMMENTARIES ON VITAL ISSUES
FOR A NEW EDUCATION

The following observations cover a variety of issues, yet they are all related to understanding psychological conditioning.

Like the seemingly random movement of life, there is no particular logical order to these observations. For the most part, they were written spontaneously while intently pondering the complexities of conditioned thinking. If one is really interested and keeps alert, then the subtleties of daily life are revealed through observation. Like the scientist patiently observing animal behavior or nature, one observes one's own nature and the structure of one's thinking and behavior.

It is not reading about conditioning or the ability to cleverly debate the issue that is important, but rather the *seeing* of conditioning within society — in media, religious persuasion, cultural idiosyncrasy, nationalistic and sentimental fervor — and the willingness to look inwardly at the source of conditioning within the psyche itself.

THE QUALITY OF ATTENTION
IN LEARNING

When the mind is quiet,
when there is no resistance to living,
when the mind is not troubled
by fearful thinking,
then one can listen,
one can love.

Children are told by their parents and teachers
to listen, to pay attention. But what is really being
asked? Generally it is for children to do something
adults want them to do. In other words, the
demand for attention has a motive. Can there be a
listening, a state of attention without a motive? Is
there any significance in being attentive, listening
without a motive?

Usually the teacher demands the child's
attention in an effort to get that child to learn
something; the child often resists. So, the teacher
speaks sharply to the child, using the voice of
authority to request that the child obey. This
happens in most schools. The child is coerced into
memorizing boring information, and when the
child resists, pressure is applied to conform. This
struggle goes on year after year, generation after
generation. It is also the struggle of parent and
child.

We may feel that the child needs to be forced
to obey, and to absorb certain information so he
can live in a complex society. Some knowledge is
obviously important and requires the child to pay

attention in order for learning to take place. But to what extent should learning be imposed? How much information does a child require? What are we asking of the child? Are children resisting the conditioning they intuitively feel is taking place as they are being educated?

If we want to rear healthy and happy children, it is imperative that we see what we are doing. If we carry on the tradition of education from generation to generation without questioning the underlying intent, we will never see the "hidden curriculum." Is socialization, the polite word for conditioning, really necessary? Are we aware of what we are doing? Have we ever asked these questions of ourselves?

A state of attention, of listening without resistance, occurs when the child feels free and open. Isn't this state of attention, of listening without a motive, the foundation of a sane behavior and a creative mind? When the mind is quiet and untroubled by fearful thinking, when there is no resistance to living, then one can listen, one can love. Or is this wishful thinking?

LEARNING THAT HAS NO MOTIVE

The child's mind,
undisturbed by the conditioning
of fearful, neurotic, convoluted thinking,
is already sane.

When we ask a child to concentrate on the task at hand, what are we asking? When learning math or biology, the child needs to concentrate his attention on that subject matter to the exclusion of all else, not to be distracted but to limit his awareness to a single point. Concentration is the narrowing of attention to a particular, and is sometimes needed when learning a subject.

But is there a difference between concentration, this single-pointed awareness, and focus? *Focus* is usually thought of as the ability to concentrate, and *concentration* is to put one's attention on one thing at a time: there is a motive, a fixed time bound view. Is there a focus that has no motive, no outward fixed point in time? Is there a focus that has no center, no inward fixed point in time? Concentration has both an outward and inward fixed point; the inward motive comes from the desire to look, stimulated by the outward objective. This process occurs within time, through effort.

The profound experience of *focus* is a heightened state of alertness when the brain has temporarily suspended mental activity. Time as we know it has ended, and there is no identification, no thing, or mental labeling of this or that. We have all had moments of timelessness, but we usually dismiss them as vagueness or inattention. Our frantic lives perpetuate constant mental activity, and thus we live out of thought day and night, never resting.

The ground of our being, living beyond thought, is rarely touched in our self-centered lives. We concentrate on our thoughts and the products of our thoughts, all of the projections and extensions of me, my, mine. How can we help the child to retain profound alertness, that timeless quality of being? The child's mind, undistorted by fearful, neurotic, convoluted thinking, is already sane. We are born without the burden of formulated ideas about life.

Can overemphasis on concentration develop a mind that is neurotic? Is our conventional educational system promoting a highly intellectual brain, one full of knowledge but isolated from living and therefore destructive? Can we enquire into the need to develop a balanced, sane mind, one capable of rational thinking and, at the same time, free from thinking?

PRISONERS OF FREEDOM

*We have created an unfree world
trying to be free.*

We speak of freedom in education and child
rearing and the freedom that a child needs to live a
happy life. We have many images of freedom. Freedom may mean we are free to say what we want, to
worship in any way we choose, to be educated in a
variety of ways, and so on. In the United States of
America, these freedoms have become our rights
and we feel that they must be protected. Globally,
each nation, each religious fragment, each group
asserts their particular freedoms, their particular
rights, with the result of creating global conflict
and lack of freedom.

So what is freedom? Can each person assume,
as his right, the freedom to do exactly as he
pleases? We are so conditioned to fight for our
freedom that we do not see the paradox. We have
created an unfree world trying to be free.

Freedom is associated with independence. The
United States of America was founded on the right
to independence as a reaction to being governed
unjustly by Great Britain. The belief in independence is deeply ingrained in Americans; they must
be independent, free individuals. But is this really
freedom? Does asserting rights bring freedom?
Does being independent bring freedom? Does
emphasizing the individual bring freedom? These
questions stir in us reactions to being unfree:
images of a socialist or communist state, a

totalitarian, limited way of life where everyone is in bondage. But are we only reacting to the fear of lack of freedom? In some parts of the world, people react adversely to freedom; they fear being out of control. So, some people consider no control to be freedom and desirable, while others consider control to be the only way and that freedom is chaos.

If we agree that freedom is to valued, what is real freedom? Surely it is to be free from the destructive influences of psychological conditioning, to be free of fragmentary thinking and the conflict of ideals. Being truly free comes when one has gone deeply within to uncover the very roots of conflict. Real freedom is not a right or a privilege to be legislated, nor is it a matter of politics, religion, economics, or any manifestation of thinking. Real freedom is when the mind is free of self-centered activity and the desire to be or to become. Can we teach our children about real freedom? Or are we going to mindlessly assert our traditional right to "freedom," our superficial tribal notions of independence?

DEATH AND THE UNKNOWN

If death is the unknown,
why do we fear
what we do not know?

What is death? Is it important to discuss this issue with young children? For a time I worked for Home Hospice, an organization dedicated to helping the terminally ill die comfortably, and there I confronted the reality of death. During my work, I talked with a group of junior high school students who were very interested in talking about death, and they shared many experiences about dying relatives. Very few adults ever take the time to discuss death except in romantic or quasi-religious terms, promising an afterlife, or heaven and hell, or some such belief. But what if we just look at the fact of death, not what we think it should be or what we hope may come after death, but just look at the reality of death?

I remember caring for one woman who was dying. After she died, I went to the funeral home; there were only a few people there, mainly the family, since the actual funeral wasn't until the next day. I remember walking up to the casket. I had only seen one dead person before and that was from a distance when I was young. As I looked down at this woman, I saw a new person; her face was totally relaxed and free of the terrible pain she had been suffering for so long. I put out my hand and touched hers; her hands were ice cold. I wondered if she would open her eyes and look at me or suddenly sit up.

Standing there, I was confronted by the *fact* of death. It was a reality. There were no images of heaven or hell in my mind, or any such creation of imaginative thinking. There was just a body that was cold. I remember thinking, "So this is death! This is all it is!"

Why are we so afraid of death? Why does the mind invent fantasies of life after death? When I taught psychology at a community college in Northern California, we talked about death, among other issues. I asked the students to take out a piece of paper and write at the top of the paper, "Death is..." Then I asked them to free-associate, to write down what came to mind when confronted with this subject. After a while we discussed their answers: "Death is like a big door closing." "Death is the end!" "Death is utter darkness." "Death is when God punishes you for your sins." My request received a wide variety of responses. Then I asked them to answer the question, "How do you know the above to be true?" Usually there was a noticeable silence and pause.

It became clear that the brain is conditioned with certain images about death. If death is the unknown, why do we fear what we do not know? Or are we really fearing the known; that is, the images we have been taught about death?

Since we are afraid of the images of death and not death itself, what reaction does fear produce in us? Do we feel threatened? What or who in us feels threatened? Do we seek security in beliefs based on our fears caused by feeling threatened?

If we looked at the fact of death directly, we would see it for what it is: nothing. We would also notice that we fear our projections of "darkness," "a big door," or "an avenging God." It's like having a bad dream; either one continues to assert that the dream is real, or one sees that the dream only exists in the mind. But there is a deeper issue in all this: "Who or what is the maker of these images?" and "Why are they made?" I am concerned with the structure of this process, to find what lies behind our fears.

Something in us feels threatened at the thought of death and, in reaction, seeks solace from this threat. Are we then establishing a maze of beliefs to justify or rationalize the fear of death? Do we create religions that promise us life after death, an endless joyful experience without all the pain of living?

In other words, the images the brain holds about death are created out of fear and if we react to fear by plunging ourselves into beliefs, then we create more conflict. Observe the endless stream of thoughts that arise in the brain. Is there an awareness that is not identified with thinking, that sees thinking for what it is? Then what is death? Isn't it the ending of the known, the culmination of all our thoughts and images, including those we have about death? When we see that our concepts about death are only thoughts we have, projections from our conditioned thinking, then can the very fear of death in us die?

THE MEANING OF SUFFERING

Is suffering compounded
by trying to get rid of suffering?

What is suffering? We all suffer, it seems. Life is full of pain, the agony of daily living with all its contradictions. Someone dies and we grieve; we feel the pain of the loss, a natural response to the death of someone we love. We also suffer from diseases: the physical body is in pain, and we hurt. So, suffering is a part of life.

Is there a deeper, more prolonged suffering we feel? When we are lonely, depressed, isolated, or fearful, we suffer. We are not loved, no one pays attention to us, we feel unworthy. If someone says they love us and then goes off with someone else, we feel rejected. Suffering is more than a response to the loss of a loved one, more than the agony of physical pain and disease.

Some say that we suffer because we have gone against God and pursued evil and decadent ways; we are sinners. They say that we need God's forgiveness to end our suffering. If only we believed in Him, we would find real joy and salvation. They say that a man called Jesus Christ died for our sins, and that in so doing he took on the suffering of the world.

Some of these people have developed a means by which we can be relieved of our prolonged suffering by confessing our sins and doing some sort of penance. Churches contain images of suffering, especially in the traditional Christian houses of worship. The figure of Christ is nailed to a cross, with blood coming from his crown of thorns, tears from his eyes, a wound in his side, his hands and feet bleeding from nails pounded through them. All this suffering! Is this terrible image of suffering meant to evoke guilt that He died for our sins? Therefore, are we to worship Him and ask His forgiveness so that we can be released from guilt?

We create our own suffering psychologically by remembering hurt and by feeling guilty. Suffering in the prolonged sense means that we live in a maze of self-indulgent, hurtful thoughts. Is suffering in this psychological sense necessary? Why do religious leaders exploit our fears and our need for forgiveness? Does further suffering come about when we try to get rid of suffering? Or when we dwell on how we did not live up to the expectations of others? If we fundamentally understand ourselves, can there be an end to this prolonged suffering?

THE MYTH OF THE AMERICAN DREAM

Can we be free in the future?

Because I was reared in the United States of America, I have been taught to believe in "The American Dream," which promises that if I work hard, am honest, thrifty and reverent, I will be successful. The overt rewards of success are money, position and security. The American Dream includes, for example, vacations to Hawaii, large cars, a two- or three-bedroom house in the suburbs, and the opportunity to make increasing financial gains. I can even become President, if I just try hard enough.

It is amazing how many people desperately and fervently believe in the dream, to the extent that they devote their whole working lives to jobs they hate in order to achieve this Utopian ideal. Then they can retire to Lake Whatever in their camper and fish their senior years away in a state of bliss. This fantasy is unfortunately all too common. And if they cannot make it, then they will sacrifice their lives by working themselves to death to support their children through college, or to earn the down payment for a house so their offspring can have some chance for the pot of gold at the end of the rainbow.

Why do we have dreams? Why do we think in terms of living the good life in the future? Have we been conditioned to think this way? How did this American Dream start? How do the first settlers of this country influence our thinking and behavior today? We still celebrate Thanksgiving and honor the Puritans as noble adventurers. But what has really happened between then and now? How did the puritanical work ethic develop into a hard, tightfisted, competitive attitude that affects our lives all these years later?

What a miserable life we create through our fearful attitudes and conditioned views — and then we dream of better times, a future of happiness, generosity and well-being. We cause our own unhappiness by wishful thinking that only postpones freeing ourselves from suffering now. If we are not free now, can we be free in the future? So, after all, isn't the American Dream just that... a dream? When will we wake up and see that the problem is in us and that living for a future solution through ideals only compounds and perpetuates the problem? How can we, in the education of young people, help them to see the fact that psychological suffering cannot be resolved through time, through belief, or through dreams. The lesson seems so simple, and yet we continue to live in the agony of beliefs, in the nightmare of our dream world.

THE DANGER OF SENTIMENT

Sentiment is a form of pleasure
for it seeks to arouse;
it titillates the brain
into constant pleasure seeking.

I listen to the radio and mostly hear "love" songs — one person lonely for another, someone leaving another, and so on. The lyrics are generally sentiment, words of jealousy and loneliness with music reinforcing the words.

Sentiment can be dangerous. Zealous, nationalistic anthems create a surge of feeling, sometimes driving people to emotional frenzy. There is great energy in emotion. Sentiment in songs and anthems is used in psychosocial conditioning by politicians and leaders in the armed forces. And the media uses it constantly, keeping us at an emotional pitch, with advertising using sentiment to manipulate the public to consume goods.

If we want our children to be psychologically free and healthy, they need to be aware of how their emotions can be played upon. Images and sounds can lead us to perform irrational actions. Can the child understand the difference between true feeling and sentiment, and make a clear distinction between passion produced by conditioning and passion that comes out of love for life? Sometimes it seems as if the whole of society is caught up in endless reinforcement of conditioned thinking, and that we act only out of lust and desire. The mind is being constantly stimulated by images of pleasure, with sentiment titillating the brain into constant self-indulgent activity. This is not a moral issue of right or wrong behavior. If we see what happens when the brain is caught in sentimentality and self-centered pleasure seeking, the danger becomes obvious. And this doesn't mean that we are condemning pleasure; judging pleasure or sentimentality creates shoulds and should nots, and then we are caught again in the conflict of ideals.

In educating our children, can we help them to observe, to creatively doubt the status quo? Can we get them to examine pleasure and sentimentality without judging? Judging or moralizing is the basis of religion and creates more and more misery and confusion. An intelligent understanding in no way uses or condones judgment, and so does not breed conflict.

THE HEROIC ADVERSARY

Isn't the patriot, the hero,
our paragon of virtue,
paradoxically the real enemy?

The conditioning that arouses patriotism
breeds violence. We are reared to be patriotic, to
pledge our allegiance, to serve and defend our
country against all enemies, foreign and domestic.
This form of conditioning has its roots in tribalism,
in primitive fears. Patriotism is a zealous unques-
tioning worship of country. And what, in essence,
is a country but a tribe, a group of people who
identify with each other through like-minded
images? Why do we need this tribal behavior? What
purpose does it serve? It brings sorrow because it
divides the world into fragments, my tribe versus
your tribe — with each faction brandishing its tribal
colors and donning its particular warrior garb
whenever someone oversteps tribal boundaries.

The hero is the honored patriot, but isn't he
the one who is most governed by conditioned
ideals? Isn't the patriot, the hero, our paragon of
virtue, paradoxically the real enemy? An enemy is
one who is hostile to another and brings injury or
harm. The hero upholds the fragmented nationalistic tribal intent; the patriot cherishes the image of
his country over all others.

What shall we teach our children about heroism
and patriotism? Do we want them to worship our
heroes? The way education is now, we condition
our children to follow leaders, to emulate heroes,

to conform to positive attitudes about the country and the figureheads who represent it. By so doing, we destroy their intelligence and their capacity to understand life.

THE UNITED NATIONS
A CONTRADICTION IN TERMS

*It is identification with the fragment
that prevents wholeness.*

For thousands of years, humankind has striven
for peace and order among nations and peoples.
Thousands of proposals have been offered, innu-
merable ideals tried, various Utopian plans legislated. But we are still violent and fragmented, divided
at almost every level, united only in our desire for
pleasure.

We teach children that the way to solve global
conflict is for all nations to come together to
discuss the problems of conflict. We have built a
complex of buildings and auditoriums in New York
City called the United Nations to serve as the
meeting ground of countries.

If we look simply at this entity called the
United Nations, what do we see? Certain individuals in various countries have been chosen to
represent their nations; they come to New York
as delegates to this structure designed for peace.
Yet there is still tremendous global conflict. Why
hasn't the process worked? Some say that it is
because we need more time to agree on the terms
of peace. But is there something fundamentally
wrong here? If we look at the structure of the
United Nations, we might be able to examine the
root of the problem.

First, the very name is a contradiction in
terms... united/nations. United means whole,

indivisible. Nations are fragments or divided parts. As long as there is fragmentation, there is not wholeness. This is a simple but overlooked fact. As long as each person is identified with his own country, with its separate nationalistic interests, there cannot be lasting peace. Writing eloquent documents proclaiming peace and the rights of all humankind is ineffectual and hypocritical! Worse, it perpetuates global violence under the guise of peace.

Until each person representing the different nations or fragments sees the truth of this simple fact, there will be no real peace — there will only be more confusion. When these representatives of nations realize the irony of the situation and drop their national identification, then there can be wholeness. Wholeness is already there! It is simply the identification with a fragment that prevents the experience of wholeness. There is really nothing one can *do* to bring about peace and wholeness in the world. All one can do is to *see* the fragmentation and, in seeing it, end it.

THE CONFLICT OF SELF-ESTEEM

Can we live without any images of self?

In education, we often talk about negative and positive self-images. We are aware of the destructive influence of a negative self-image, when one has a mental picture of oneself as a failure or unworthy. Educators, administrators and parents have developed programs to build self-esteem to replace the negative self-image with a positive one. The person with a positive self-image has a mental picture of himself as capable, successful and worthy. But isn't this positive self-image just as limiting as a negative one? Granted, it is more comforting to have images of success than of failure, but both images limit the person: each is a form of conditioning, and breeds conflict.

What is self-image? How does it function? A negative self-image has associated feelings of depression and isolation. Developing a positive self-image is supposed to eradicate or replace a negative one. The child is usually rewarded for certain tasks he can do well, and slowly builds a sense of self-confidence.

Confidence means belief in one's abilities. It is important that the child be able to learn, unhindered by a negative self-image. We are only questioning the intelligence of replacing the negative self-image with a positive one.

Self-image is a conclusion, a view one has drawn about oneself based on past knowledge. In order to successfully operate complicated machinery, or build bridges, or solve the challenges of science and medicine, one needs to have knowledge about the subject. And in order to gather knowledge, it helps to be vitally interested in the matter at hand. If you love doing what you do, you can bring a great deal of energy to the challenges of living. Knowledge, capability, and the love of a subject are all requisites for becoming an educated human being. So where does positive self-image come in? As stated earlier, self-image is a conclusion, a static view about one's capabilities. This conclusion is fixed in time. Although the conclusion may be built upon, it is unmoving, stationary. When one builds upon this self-image, what happens? Does one become identified with that self-image and call it "me"? When one has an image of someone else, what is one's relationship to that person? Is this image based on the past? The issue of self-image seems to have deep consequences.

When I have an image of myself and also of you, what is our relationship? If I begin to associate with others who have similar self-images, what happens when we form a collective identification based on this common image? Can we live without any images of self? Is the development and maintenance of the self-image fundamentally divisive? Are there global implications? One begins to have an insight into the root of the problem when one asks questions of a serious nature, with the interest and patience to follow through in uncovering the underpinnings of psychological conflict.

THE ROOTS OF VIOLENCE

*It is this need to defend
that isolates the mind,
divides person from person,
and separates human beings.*

I think that what causes violence is so obvious
that it escapes us. We imagine it to be a force
beyond our understanding or control, unaware that
the violence in the world is directly related to our
own internal violence, violence that is conditioned
into our daily existence. We have been educated to
look for solutions to the symptoms of violence
appearing in our "current events," daily papers,
and on television. It seems to me that concern over
symptomatic issues such as capital punishment,
nuclear weapons, or war is far removed from
examination of the causes of violence, and without
understanding the causes, we can never fundamentally eradicate violence. It will continue to plague us
as it has since the very beginning of human relationship.

One of the blocks to our understanding is that
we have come to accept violence as an inevitable
part of life. We think that perhaps we can reform a
few particularly bothersome kinds of behavior, but
we really feel that humans are inherently violent
and cannot fundamentally change. This view has
been a main factor in preventing us from ending
violence. It is a myth that must be fully explored
and exposed.

We talk endlessly about violence and look to all

sorts of experts to tell us what to do, but all the while the source of the problem is right in front of us — for it is us! The problem lies in our relationships of mutual exploitation created by fear. The fear may be residual behavior from more primitive times when tribes competed for too few resources, but today it is a different world with enough to go around. We have so much food that we stockpile, or destroy, or pay farmers not to grow — all so we can keep up a destructive contest of economic one-upmanship, so the few at the top can reap tremendous profits. When this dominant minority controls the greater bulk of the world's resources, it is inevitable that the majority at the base of the pyramid must struggle against each other for whatever is left over after the self-assertive have taken their proportional bites, and on down the pecking order.

I am not singling out the United States or free enterprise as the villain. The violence of aggression and competition is a human issue that involves everyone. Russia also has violence, though on the surface their particular form appears to be different — but violence is violence. The Communist system of political violence manifests as repression, and people are punished for not obeying the guidelines of government and a particular Utopian vision of life. Human beings in Russia, it seems to me, protect themselves through an ideological system that controls behavior. The devastation they encountered in the Second World War, the experience of being attacked and losing millions of people, made them highly sensitive to violence. As a nation they were brutally hurt, and they defend themselves from the threat of a repetition of that experience.

What I am trying to say here is that the causes of violence, in *any* economic or political scheme, appear to have their roots in universal psychological human traits — in the individualistic, self-centered exploitation of human resources; in the fearful, aggressive drive to compete and to dominate; and in the need to control human behavior through a system of conditioning and enforced belief in ideological thinking. These traits, however, are only superficial. In order to understand the cause, we must delve even deeper, to the source of social disorder.

If one looks closely at the mind, one can see how it functions; for example, how it gets hurt and how, out of this hurt, fear arises. This fear produces a need to defend, which is a creation of the protective mechanism. The need to defend isolates the individual, dividing person from person. The mind creates belief systems, based on particular conditioning, as a defense against further hurt. These belief systems, as political ideologies or religious dogma, break up the human race into factions (i.e., Arab, Jew, American, Russian, Christian, Catholic). One can observe, especially during wartime, each side believing that what they are doing is correct and just. The mind itself, hurt and fearful, wants to change itself so as to live free of pain. It tries to change by creating more ideals, denying the hurt, and affecting a more positive behavior. This does not help; in fact, it compounds the problem by creating conflict between the fact of hurt and the ideal of "nonhurt" (well-being), or socially between the fact of violence and the ideal of nonviolence.

So, as I see it, the root causes of violence are seated in the fundamental workings of the mind, how it gets hurt and how it deals with this hurt. If one seriously traced violence from its symptoms to its source, one would eventually arrive at the individual human psyche. Instead, people look for relief in the mind's inappropriate responses to hurt — in ideologies, ideals, defensive reactions. The problem is fragmentation, for the mind has created a world broken up into separate, isolated belief systems because it does not understand how to deal with the basic problem of hurt. It should also be obvious that our conventional fragmentary approaches to solving the problem of violence cannot work. A good example is the United Nations. How can a collection of fragments called "nations," each one consisting of a group of individuals psychologically identified with a particular belief system, be united or whole? How can there be cooperation when there is division? The United Nations is a contradiction in terms. Religions suffer the same divisiveness.

The only way for us to make sense out of this world is to realize that real cooperation requires each person to understand how he or she contributes to the problem by being a fragmented human. When this is understood, then each person, by rejecting any fragmentary way of living, can be whole and therefore end violence at its core. In other words, in order to end violence, to be whole,

to live without conflict, to cooperate in relationship, one would have to end fragmentation since
fragmentation caused by hurt and fear is at the root
of violence.

The symptoms of our violence are apparent in
almost everything we do. In this part of the world,
under our particular Capitalistic ideological system,
advertising or marketing in business is a vivid
symptom of violence. This means of indoctrinating
the mind into consuming, "buying into the belief,"
is an excellent place to start a serious investigation
into the deeper roots of violence. First, one must
go beneath the surface of the political, economic,
sociological network. Secondly, one must be free of
any belief system. If one has a vested interest in any
system, then one cannot look unbiasedly. Even the
reformers can become a part of mutual exploitation, because their vested interest is to perpetuate
themselves as experts; they use opposition to the
violence created by hurt and fear as a means of self-
aggrandizement so that they can personally get
ahead.

In essence, violence has its roots in the
reaction of the psyche to being hurt; fear becomes
defensiveness, leading to isolated self-image,
fragmentation, division and, finally, conflict. The
traditional approach to understanding violence has
been superficial and has led, paradoxically, to the
compounding of violence through the creation of
ideals, beliefs and systems to control behavior —
and it does not matter whether those ideals, beliefs
or systems are political, religious, or philosophical.
Belief simply reinforces defensiveness, and

intensifies fear and hurt. The only sensible approach is to see how the mind is hurt and to observe its responses to that hurt. This seeing, or observation, is *insight.* Insight that can end hurt comes about by observing hurt, not moving away from it; rather one sees that *any* action taken to deal with hurt is a fragmentary reaction, and only compounds the problem by creating more violence. This is not an intellectual approach. It is not a new philosophy, religion, or psychological gimmick. We simply need to look deeply at the root of violence, at its source — in the functioning of the human psyche. I am not asserting this to be true but am, rather, putting it forth for us to look at. Either there is a fundamental cause of violence, or there isn't.

THE DANGER OF BECOMING ONE HUMANITY

Demon es Deus Invertus...
The Devil is God inverted.

The usual process in trying to bring about a change in human behavior is to deny the negative or undesirable quality one wants to change and affirm the positive or desirable quality one wants to attain. We look towards finding out what we should be doing, and do not look at what we actually do. We judge our behavior and, consequently, bring about conflict in the name of reform, in the name of idealism.

This process occurs in numerous ways. One way that has been tried in an attempt to bring about a global response to changing the violent nature of humanity is to affirm our "connectedness," our commonality, to see that underneath all our violent behavior we are really "one," and therefore we should stop hurting ourselves.

Countless articles have been written about being positive, connected, becoming one humanity. But isn't this wishful thinking when, in fact, the world is not one humanity? The world is in continual conflict due to our separateness. So many idealistic reformers think that all we need to do is see our oneness and we will stop being violent towards each other, that humankind will join hands in one loving mass of mutual cooperation. Governments have even gone so far as to create "oneness laws," so that we are forced to embrace the group consciousness. Religiously inclined people find their oneness through mutual belief in an all pervasive God, a force that will adhere our beings into one global whole. All this seems romantic, fanciful, and terribly simplistic.

Why don't we look directly at the violence that separates us? Have we judged violence in order to change it? Judgment, the process of thought used to change behavior, conditions us through the powerful reinforcement of negative associations. It hurts to look at ourselves; the pain of self-consciousness prevents us from looking at what we do. Our so-called conscience, the moral guidelines instilled in us, is basically judgment; it says that what we do is "bad" and what we should be doing is "good."

The ugliness of human suffering is not something to linger over. I personally do not think it does us any good to dwell on battle casualties, car accidents, and other catastrophies. I do not consider "current events" either current or educational. Atrocities have been going on since the beginning of human relationship; there is nothing new about man's inhumanity to man. The news just adds to the statistics, adding misery to misery — a macabre scorekeeping.

I define something as educational if it enlightens one to the facts of a problem so one can intelligently understand and resolve it. In order to prepare us to solve problems, a true education must reach to the causal level, so that the problem is seen at its root and, therefore, can be prevented from happening agair Anything short of prevention at the root level is reform, which is not based on understanding why or how we do something.

Dwelling on the manifestations of our separateness is morose and unenlightening, but if we look at the fundamental psychological causes, we are approaching the problem from an entirely different perspective. If we look at what separates us, we would paradoxically find a desperate need to discover our common humanity.

Many people state that to discover what connects human beings is a logical approach to peace. Human beings have been attempting this for thousands of years; it is the basis of religious, political and philosophical thought aimed at bringing about cooperation and unity between people. The process is commonly called "idealism," and the desired ideal state of "connectedness" or "oneness" has been called God, Buddha, Christ, Energy, Harmony, Love, and even "The Force." On a more mundane level, idealism focuses on human similarities rather than on those traits that make us different. It is an "accentuate the positive and eliminate the negative" approach. However, I think that this approach, however noble, is a way that paradoxically brings about and sustains the negative. In other words, any action to "discover our connections," our "oneness," or to bring about the positive is idealistic, and by its very nature brings about conflict, misery, and suffering.

The process of discovering our "connections" or our "commonality" creates separateness because it aims to influence our behavior towards that connection or commonality. The *fact* is that we are separate. The *hope* is that we are connected, that somehow, underneath our separateness, there is unity. The problem occurs when we *try* to become connected. This process of becoming — that is, setting up ideals — causes division. A fact is a fact and an ideal is illusion, a form of wishful thinking. To set up an ideal, or a "what should be," to replace fact creates conflict — between the fact (what is) and the ideal (what should be). The harder one tries to attain the ideal, any ideal, the more one has to get rid of the fact, to eliminate the problem. But one's efforts only seem to create a tension in oneself and, hence, externally in the world. Anything divided within itself, fragmented, is in a state of conflict.

There is a Latin saying, "Demon est Deus Invertus" meaning "The Devil is God Inverted," which implies that the Devil or evil is created by the creation of the good or God. In other words, to try to eliminate the problem of human separateness by the creation of an ideal — such as the search for our commonality or connectedness — is a process of conflict. The only way I know to solve the problem that does not compound it by setting up ideals is to realize that to understand any situation, one has to look at the facts only. If my car is not working well, what should I do? Do I search for the ideal car — or do I stop, open the hood, and begin to observe what has gone mechanically awry? I think that human problems require the same approach, but that our vanity prevents us from seeing ourselves as ordinary or mechanistic. We tend to view ourselves as lofty beings, surely not mere creatures of habit and commonplace error, subject to operant conditioning.

In essence, I am saying that our need to discover mutual connectedness arises from human suffering caused by our separateness and is itself the very action that creates the disconnectedness or separateness! Perhaps the supposed underlying connectedness or commonality is nothing more than our own self-centered projection. It is ironic that by trying desperately to bring about wholeness and harmony, we create fragmentation and disharmony.

I think that in order to be connected, paradoxically, one has to be completely alone. Being totally alone, not seeking anything, a person can be "all one," a real individual. The word *individual* originally meant indivisible, whole, not capable of being separated. If one is intrinsically whole, indivisible within one's psyche, then there is no *need* to be connected with others. But when we *try* to be whole through will power, through the need to create a sense of external unity, we fragment ourselves and create separateness in our desire to be connected with others. I do not see how wholeness can come about by "discovering our connectedness" outside ourselves. Only when we perceive and put aside this striving to be connected does separation dissolve.

People separate themselves because of their ambitions. The ambition to succeed, to win as individuals ("individualism"), encourages "each person for himself." Psychologically isolated in our separate ego structures, we are divided. Divided, we are pitted one against another to ensure our own survival. We perpetuate this thrust for individual survival in education; we teach our children to become successful, competitive, isolated, fragmented human beings. Then, once we are separated and feel the pain of that, we covet wholeness, and our ambition turns towards achieving unity with others.

Why can't we see what we are doing? How did we set up this incredible relationship of mutual exploitation based on separation? We create a situation, then label it bad, and sustain the badness by creating its opposite, the ideal of goodness.

PATRIOTISM
THE ENEMY OF PEACE

*The clinging for security to the nation
and the patriotic zeal to remember
and identify with the heroic war dead
are the very actions that
create and sustain violence!*

Patriotism and nationalism hold terrible contradictions. Patriots believe that peace comes from upholding the honor of their nation, and fervently believe that they must cherish the nation's past and glorify their war dead. They keep these memories alive through ceremonies, heroic images, and terrifying displays of armed force.

People have been psychologically scarred by wars. Both Russians and Americans remember the last great war with fear. Being afraid, they protect and isolate themselves inwardly and outwardly; the nature of fear is isolating. Inwardly, the mind creates defenses against being hurt in the future. It holds on to memory, the past, resolving that these terrible things shall never happen again. In this fear and defensiveness, the mind projects outwardly and creates external defenses. It clings to the familiar, the security of its people, its culture, nation, and builds barriers around itself. We think that by clinging for security to that which is greater than us, we will survive. But the opposite is true. The clinging for security to the nation, and the zeal to remember and identify with the heroic war dead, are the very actions that create and sustain violence. In other words, the conventional approach to bringing about "peace" through patriotic or nationalistic identification is, paradoxically, the essence of war because it is based on fear and isolating, self-protective thinking.

Almost everyone is caught up in identifying with the greater symbol, with the fragmentary, nationalistic perspective. Russians fear the Americans and Americans fear the Russians; Arabs fear the Israelis and Israelis fear the Arabs; and so on. Each is identifying with the fragment, projecting that the other is the enemy, and creating higher and higher walls of isolation and resistance. We try through social reform to end the isolation, to bring down the walls, but all we really seem to do is create further barriers. We do not see that the problem cannot be dealt with through reform because it is rooted in the human brain. The self-centered need for psychological survival generates the need to identify and formulate belief systems for security. The fundamental fear that produces nationalistic identification and, hence, isolation has its roots in individualistic thinking — that "I" must survive above all. The Socialist or Communist view is that conformity to the group or nation is all important, and in the West individual success is worshipped. Both views are based on particular cultural conditioning, perspectives that are imposed upon the brain out of fear and belief and arise from the same source. We continue to look outwardly for the answer to conflict in relationship, not realizing that the very eyes through which we look are the source of the problem, that in trying to mold the world to our beliefs, to our fearful self-protective views, we destroy it in the process.

Perhaps we are too used to indulging ourselves in romantic political causes or noble religious quests to look at the actual mundane reality of our behavior. Since focus on social reform, on the symptom, is familiar, can we look at this in a new light? Perhaps we can start from where we actually are, but with new vision. We must first shift our perspective from trying to change the problem of conflict to wanting to *understand* it. We must suspend our usual approach and seriously question conventional ways of bringing about peace. It is vital that we become aware of the tragic irony in patriotism and nationalism, and see that the very actions we believe will save us and bring about peace are the very actions that destroy us. We need to understand that trying to achieve national security by honoring the memory of past wars and war dead is what sustains fear and, in so doing, builds greater barricades to understanding, creating further isolation, fragmentation, division and, hence, conflict. It is the very act of prevention that is, paradoxically, the cause of violence.

Can we see that there can never be wholeness, real world peace, if there is fragmentation — my country versus your country, my ideal versus your ideal? The only way this could work is if one belief dominated the world, converting every human being to its ways... which is what many have tried to do. Each country is determined that their way is

---

best, each religious fragment that they are the "chosen one." Are we aware of the potential violence and tremendous arrogance inherent in this way of thinking? Politicians and religious leaders propose to bring about world order and peace. This is an ideal. Through fragmentary political or religious beliefs, what they are actually doing is creating a divided, violent world at war. It appears that mankind does not really want harmony. Our intellectual ideals speak eloquently of peace and yet our actions are violent, self-centered and divisive. We are hypocrites; we say "love thy neighbor" but we fear him. We build walls of resistance around ourselves and huddle together in small bands, terrified that others ("they") will attack us. It seems that we are still very primitive, warlike tribes in a modern jungle. Our weapons, no longer sticks or stones, are capable of killing millions of people in a matter of seconds. And the way we are going about trying to solve the problem of violence is itself violent.

CAN THINKING SOLVE THE PROBLEMS THINKING HAS CREATED?

*Can thinking critique itself,
enquire into its own workings?*

Today, there are many "new" ways of thinking — psychological, philosophical, religious, political, economic, sociological, biological, anthropological, and historical — and many new theories exist about the reasons for global conflict and suffering. In "new" thinking in psychology, the mind has invented an endless array of approaches to human development, taking the study of the act of living to a new and more complex state-of-the-art. It seems that to be "self-actualized" (humanistic psychology's noble ideal), or "self-transcended" (transpersonal psychology's lofty goal), the average person would need to spend his life and then some devoted to the overwhelming "spiritual paths" of attainment.

Do we really believe that all this "new" thinking is bringing about order, or is it producing more confusion and disorder? Have we ever stopped to examine this process fundamentally? What are we trying to do with all this "new" thinking? Have we fallen in love with the process of thinking as the end-all? Have we considered if thinking can actually solve conflict? Granted, thinking can solve scientific and technological problems, and functions efficiently in this area; however, scientific thinking can also become self-centered and distorted, creating destructive technological solutions and devices.

The single fundamental question is: "Can thinking solve the problems thinking has created?" If we take this question seriously, then perhaps we might approach the solving of conflict in a radically new way. The purpose of this book is to examine, not answer, this question. It is a part of our overeducated, conditioned approach to expect answers. Can we, instead, just hold on to the question, so to speak, and begin to become aware of the process of thinking itself, how it functions in *both* the technological and psychological realms? Can thinking critique itself, enquire into its own workings? This is not an intellectual process. We are asking if we can actually witness thought in action, watching its movement in us each moment. Being aware of how thinking becomes manifest in the world, we may be able to see how thinking creates social structures which reinforce its place in society.

It seems that creating "new" ways of thinking only sustains the problem. Is there actually a "new" way of thinking, or is an age-old process re-dressed in modern clothing to appear fresh and new? If this is the case, then it is not inventing another "new" way of thinking, but rather understanding the old way, that leads to freedom.

THE MYTH OF MANY PATHS

*For conflict to end,
do we need to end belief?*

We are conditioned to be tolerant of all people, to accept the incongruity of humanity, to embrace the diverse ways people choose to believe and live. In essence, we believe that all paths lead to the same source, but have we really looked at this or have we just accepted it as true because of our own personal, particular way or belief system? That one person's influence should dominate or that one belief system should prevail is what humans have been trying to effect for thousands of years. Human beings have individually and collectively tried to influence behavior through political and religious indoctrination, to sway people into believing in their particular dogma or creed to gain power and influence. But have we ever questioned the need to believe, or fundamentally questioned what purpose belief serves?

Many people assert that belief brings people together, but is this really true? Isn't it actually the nature of belief to separate, divide and, hence, create conflict? Some say that to bring about wholeness, we need to honor *all* beliefs, thereby creating unity in diversity. But are we fooling ourselves?

Why are we so afraid to face life directly? Why do we hide in intellectual, romantic escapes? Are we afraid of seeing pain, suffering and disorder, so we escape into beliefs? Do we actually need the comfort and security that beliefs seem to provide us?

Democratic nations pride themselves on tolerance and freedom — their cherished ideals — but, in actuality, are the people tolerant or free? Or are they, in their daily lives, caught up in isolating and fragmentary beliefs?

Democratic nations pride themselves on "rights": the right to free speech, the right to worship as one pleases, and so on. Doesn't this demand for rights come out of a reaction to being forced to believe, to conform to a particular pattern of behavior? Does having a "right" to believe bring freedom or, paradoxically, lead to more of the same — more conditioned thinking and living?

There are those who say that their right to believe comes directly from God, the Ultimate Authority. Does this intimidate people from questioning? Isn't this another trick of the mind to convert others to its deductions through authoritative persuasion?

Many kindhearted people believe that someday in the future people will come together under one God and live without conflict. This is called "hope" or "faith." But can conflict end in the future? Are we not evading the fact that conflict is actually sustained now by this type of thinking? In other words, hope and faith breed conflict, isolation, and division because this approach is in time and therefore incapable of bringing about fundamental change now.

Can we examine if what we call "paths" are actually illusions based on the hope that one day we will be free? This is not a negative question. Most people fear facing the truth of something because they have judged it. Judgment brings pain and keeps us from looking directly at the facts, therefore preventing us from understanding and going beyond judgment.

How ironic that the very actions we take to bring about "positive" behavior, wholeness, peace, and order in actuality bring about the opposite! How can each of us, individually or collectively, become identified with like-minded others, maintain our separate beliefs, and also bring about unity in the world? Some say that if we believe in wholeness, have an image of unity and visualize world peace, conflict can end. But for conflict to end, don't we need to end belief? Have we approached the ending of conflict in the wrong way? We tenaciously cling to our beliefs, seeing them as inseparable from ourselves, because without belief we feel life will be meaningless and not worth living. So, we continue trying to bring "meaning" to our lives by our beliefs and, therefore, sustain conflict.

We believe in symbols of world peace and mesmerize ourselves into thinking and feeling that we are doing good work, when in actuality we are creating a world of disorder and violence. If we could only look at this without rejecting or judging, we would see the truth of something, which is actuality and not negative at all! Yet the mind conjures up fears and continues in its own dream world. What prevents us from seeing the truth of this is the holding to individual paths and separate (or all-encompassing) belief systems. Opinion, intellectual debates, and the stimulation of differing views sustain the individual (ego). We seem to thrive on conflict and get tremendous vitality and energy from opposition.

It seems that we really do not want to be at peace and tenaciously defend our ways, paths, and beliefs, for in this separation we find our place and meaning in life.

POLITICS
THE ART OF CONFLICT

Can conflict end in the future?

Conflict is produced because our system of politics is founded on opposition and separatism. As humans, we seem to thrive on conflict, the battle of wills, and all the drama this produces. Our lives are based on competition and winning. If there were no conflict, what would we do? If we could not compete, what would be the fun in living?

Some say that conflict creates growth and is a positive force in learning. They say that new meaning and approaches arise out of conflict. Many feel that life would be dull without conflict and, in this way, glorify our separateness, individual attainments, and personal dreams and fulfillments. They assert that the probable truth is that without conflict we would be nothing.

Does conflict produce real change and growth? Growth means time, change that occurs in the future. Can conflict end in the future, through a step by step process of attaining life without conflict?

Politics are intended to produce social well-being. How can we have social well-being when our political parties are in opposition from the start? It appears that differentness and opposition benefit the self-fulfilling candidate and his like-minded followers. In other words, politics require and sustain personal gain and power.

Political conventions are superficial displays of sensationalism and sentiment, vulgar and petty exhibitions of people's need for identification. We need to help students understand such primitive political ritual so they can make rational, intelligent decisions regarding the serious challenges of life.

THE ENDING OF WAR
AN HOLISTIC APPROACH

People have spent lifetimes
in superficial explorations
into the nature of war.

War has been going on for thousands of years; people have killed millions of their own kind. Volumes have been written about war and its causes, historically, sociologically and psychologically. War has been, and continues to be, humankind's solution to solving conflict. Why? Can we ask this question simply, holistically?

In order to stop war, we must first stop warring! It is obvious that we must end the solving of conflict by violent means if we want to end violence. But this is only the beginning of ending violence, for the roots of war are far deeper. However, the first and most obvious realization is at the political or symptomatic level.

To explore the causes of war, we must go below the brutality of overt aggression to the second level and question our conventional *approaches* to bringing about peace to see if they are, in fact, producing the opposite effect. Are religious and political institutions that are dedicated to the peaceful resolution of conflict actually inducing violence? Does religious thinking bring peace or does it, through the imposition of ideals, create personal and social conflict? Do politics generate well-being and order in society or, being based on opposition, create disorder and competitive aggression? We must seriously question our traditional views in this area, but we also need to go beyond this second sociological, symptomatic level to the deepest roots of conflict.

In order to examine the ending of war holistically, on every level, we will need to enquire into the cause of war at the psychological level, the level of the human psyche, to see how conflict is fundamentally created there through conditioned beliefs and the use of thinking to change behavior.

Too often we have only touched the first level, getting lost in a maze of confused, symptomatic thinking, writing volumes about this particular war or that particular war. People have spent lifetimes in superficial explorations into the nature of war but rarely has anyone gone beneath the surface, except in moralistic discourse. Rarely has anyone questioned the conventional approaches to resolving conflict, and even more rare is the person who goes beyond that into the roots of psychological and social disorder.

CREATIVE DISCONTENT

Doubt and discontent
are vital ingredients
in a psychological revolution
in learning.

Why are we so concerned with success and the images of success? It seems that the underlying purpose of our conventional education is to condition young people to succeed, to develop the affectations of success. What is this so-called confidence that we seem to want, the image of savoir-faire? Can we observe this behavior in ourselves, or see it in others, without becoming identified with it?

The confidence of the business person, the swaggering, mock-friendly attitude he gives out; the confidence of the politician or national leader playing with power; the confidence of the religious leader whose only authority is God; the confidence of the educator with his control over the lives of children; the confidence of an expert in the academic world — is this confidence or bravado? Real self-esteem or facade? I do not deny that professionalism or expertise have value, but the professional image or persona that one develops to give the air of casual confidence is often empty, false.

It is important to help our children see through this vanity. We need to foster in them a sense of creative doubt, a questioning attitude, so that young people are not fooled by the superficiality of the self-image that projects a false sense of confidence. We need to help them be creatively discontent with the way things are. Doubt can help free the child from the influences of conditioning. Doubt does not unquestioningly accept the conventional; discontent can break up the rigid patterns of traditional behavior without rebellion. Creative doubt and discontent are vital ingredients in a psychological revolution in learning and are necessary qualities for a healthy and sane life.

AFTERWORD
Where Do We Go From Here?

We have explored the structure of psychological conditioning; examined the nature of enquiry and intelligence; looked at a new education with the basic goal of understanding psychological conditioning; and we have shared observations on a variety of issues related to sane and intelligent living, including a sample curriculum for educators and parents. I want to stress again that the intent of this book, and all others in this series, is to stimulate enquiry and to provide a direction for looking at these subjects *ourselves*. These books are not written as intellectual dissertations; nor do they treat the history of educational reform. The philosophy or psychological perspective is not new, and yet to see these matters directly is always fresh and new.

This series of books is concerned with a psychological revolution in learning. *Revolution* is a highly conditioned word. Historically it means war, conflict, a violent overthrow of a government. However, I am using the word revolution to mean a complete change — not through force or coercion, but through intelligence and fundamental under-standing of the roots of the psychological disorder within ourselves and the world that is termed "psychological conditioning." This fundamental understanding of ourselves will eventually affect the structures created in society by conditioned thinking. There need be no violent overthrow of the status quo; change will occur without physical confrontation or use of military strength.

This psychological revolution involves a radical shift in human behavior. As it is now, learning is primarily the accumulation of information and the analysis of that knowledge to bring about change. In science and technology, this method is appropriate. However, learning through analysis is also being used on human beings to change their behavior; we are challenging this learning method as applied to psychological problems. As we have said before, changing human behavior through analysis and judgment (and thereby creating ideals) is, paradoxically, a process that creates violence and disorder, both inwardly and outwardly.

A psychological revolution in learning approaches the changing of behavior in a completely new way, disregarding all the superficial reforms of politics, economics, and religion. This fundamental reform penetrates to the root of thinking itself, which is why it is a radical revolution.

The intent of this series of books is to bring about an understanding of psychological conditioning, to alert readers to its danger, and to arouse interest in developing schools and educational environments that focus on this purpose. For centuries we have ventured along a potentially self-destructive path in education. We need to notice our own road to destruction and the violence that is its foundation. Once one sees this, there is the possibility of immediate change. Our conditioning may come back the next moment, but if we remain aware and carefully observe each movement of conditioned thinking, then conditioning can end in that observation.

It is not cumulative learning that ends conditioning. In fact, the accumulation of information and attitudes is what constitutes conditioned learning and becomes the psychologically conditioned content of our consciousness. This accumulation is what we want to bring an end to, not perpetuate; it is the source of our problems. Immediate learning from observation — that is, learning which is not cumulative — is *insight* or *intelligence*. This intelligent learning can bring about a psychological revolution in our education, a completely new course of action in bringing about order and well-being in living. It requires us to have the passion to change; we must feel the urgency!

Where is the passion that will give us the energy to effect change? Has our passion been sapped by the constant pursuit of pleasure? Do we really feel the danger of psychological conditioning? Do we actually see how it affects us, individually and collectively? Do we feel an intense need to bring about a psychological revolution in our thinking? Or are we too caught up in intellectual speculation, conjecture, opinions and conclusions to *see* how dangerous our way of life is? Perhaps we are too highly educated to see the obvious dangers inherent in our way of living.

If we can truly see the simple truth of how we create violence in the way that we condition our children and ourselves, then we can break our association with that way of life. We can step out of the tremendous momentum of "the same old way"

by questioning ourselves and developing schools
and environments based on the understanding of
psychological conditioning.

Where do we go from here?
If we really see the problem,
the answer is there.

Photo: Earl Bates

Terrence Webster-Doyle was Founder and Director of three independent schools and has taught at the secondary, community college and university levels in Education, Psychology and Philosophy. He has worked in Juvenile Delinquency Prevention and has developed counseling programs for teenagers. He has earned a doctorate degree in Psychology, has produced numerous conferences and workshops on New Directions in Education, and was the Director of The Center for Educational Alternatives in Northern California. Currently, he is Co-director of a secondary school whose intent is to explore psychological conditioning, and is working on a series of children's books exploring the same theme.

ABOUT THE PUBLISHER

Atrium Publications concerns itself with fundamental issues which prevent understanding and cooperation in human affairs. Starting with the fact that our minds are conditioned by our origin of birth, education, and experiences, Atrium Publications' intent is to bring this issue of conditioning to the forefront of our awareness. Observation of the fact of conditioning, becoming directly aware of the movement of thought and action, brings us face-to-face with the actuality of ourselves. Seeing who we actually are, not merely what we think we are, reveals the potential for a transformation of our ways of being and relating.

If you would like more information, please write or call us. We enjoy hearing from people who read our books and appreciate your comments.

Published by:
Atrium Publications
Post Office Box 938
Ojai, California 93023
(805) 646-0488
or (800) 432-5566 for book order information

Other books written by
Terrence Webster-Doyle

For Adults

• **Growing Up Sane**:
Understanding the Conditioned Mind

• **One Encounter, One Chance**:
The Essence of Take Nami Do Karate*

• **Peace — The Enemy of Freedom**:
The Myth of Nonviolence

•**Karate**:
The Art of Empty Self

• **The Religious Impulse**:
A Quest for Innocence

For Young People

• **Facing the Double-Edged Sword**:
The Art of Karate for Young People**

• **Why is Everybody Always Picking on Me?**:
A Guide to Handling Bullies

• **Tug of War**:
Peace Through Understanding Conflict

• **Fighting the Invisible Enemy**:
Solving Conflict Peacefully

*Finalist: Benjamin Franklin Award — Psychology/Self-Help
**Finalist: Benjamin Franklin Award — Interior Design
Winner: Award of Excellence, Ventura Ad Society